ORGA
THE WISDOM BOOK

Isidore Friedman

Proverbs 4:7

"Wisdom is the principal thing; therefore, get wisdom; Yea, with all thy getting get understanding".

1 Kings 3: 5-15

"When the Lord came to Solomon and wanted to gratify any wish he desired, Solomon had only one wish - Wisdom and a discerning heart. The Lord granted his request and added everything else to boot - wealth, glory, peace and love".

The obvious meaning here is that when one has Wisdom one automatically has everything else.

But what is this thing called Wisdom? How does a person go about acquiring it? Where is it found? And how is it applied?

ORGANICS WISDOM LIBRARY
2462 Riverbluff Parkway
Sarasota, Florida 34231

Copyright© 2002 by Nancy Dahlberg
ISBN: 978-0-9657544-1-5

All rights reserved. No part of this book may be reproduced in any form or by any means, electronic or mechanical, including photocopying, recording, or by any information storage and retrieval system, without permission in writing from the publisher.

2024 Trade Paperback Edition in cooperation with:
Conscious Books. Editor: Dr. Greg Nielsen
Word-processing by: Monica P. - Fiverr
Trade Paperback Design: Ankit Todi - Fiverr

Mention of Alfred Korzybski refers his book
Science and Sanity.
Printed in the United States of America
Cover design by Joseph Polansky
Original artwork by Isidore Friedman

"Dedicated to the One Light

which is

ever new, ever fresh, ever more radiant

in every age"

The cover of this book was designed by Joseph Polonsky, Nancy Dahlberg and Dr. Greg Nielsen. It includes an original serpent drawn by the author. Isidore always drew this unique and expressive serpent inside his books and on the covers of his notebooks. It conveyed the importance and authenticity of his work and summed up many of the ideas in his teaching.

The serpent's intense and quite human look shows that we're to become "serpents of wisdom." Since the snake is a creature that sheds its skin regularly, it's also a symbol of change and psychic transformation. The serpent's triple flame represents the triune nature of the one life force in us. It alludes to our basic structure which is composed of spirit, soul, and body. It shows that we have powers of light, love, and vitality within us that we need to awaken and harmonize.

The infinity signs and the serpent's undulating body express that life is an eternal process which comes in waves and cycles. The plus and minus signs are its ever-present polarities - positive and negative forces - which create and accomplish all things. The five-pointed star represents the final goal - conscious man in control of the four elements. The serpent's upright stance reiterates this.

It stands for the awakened kundalini force which rises up along the aspirant's spine and activates his higher centers and faculties as he evolves spiritually. The serpent which once tempted him in the Garden of Eden is now the redeemer of purified and uplifted power.

- Nancy Dahlberg –

Contents

Wisdom Book Part I 7
    Chapter 1 9
    Chapter 2 15
    Chapter 3 23
    Chapter 4 31
    Chapter 5 41
    Chapter 6 47
The Wisdom Book Part II 63
Clear Thinking 105
Natural Order Notes 111
Organics For Everyday Living 117
Steps On The Path 127
Organic Notes 133
On Self Knowledge... 139
Right Speech.. 145
Some Fundamentals Of The New Age Gnosis 155
Percepton 163

THE WISDOM BOOK

PART I

1

Some Attempts At Setting Up Referents
For the Word Wisdom

STAR FIRE 21

May the Core of Light shine in your heart
That from beast ignorance you will forever part
May your mind rest deep, trained and serene
To receive your cosmic message clean.

May your Guiding Tone remove the clatter
Of your concepts dead that forever shatter
The meaning and purpose of your central life
Which lifts you above blind verbal strife.

May the Light, the Love, and the Wisdom-Power
Cleanse your mind-heart hour by hour
That, balanced understanding in you may grow
And the Light-Substance of Wisdom into you may flow.

May the One and the many in you be fed
By the Lighted Tone continually led
May balance forever guide your days
Into the higher true Gnostic Ways.

May you work in Light and rest in Peace
That conscious living in you will release
The Holy One, chained, but now set free
To measure in you Light of Eternity.

Isidore Friedman

SOME ATTEMPTS AT SETTING UP REFERENTS FOR THE word wisdom are:

- Wisdom is the ability to apply the structure-function-order coordinates of the Cosmic Process (God) in everyday living in line with the Natural Order (Life-Facts).
- Wisdom is the ability to set limits.
- Wisdom is skill in action.
- Wisdom is the application of balance, control and alternation to your daily function.
- Understanding starts with self-knowledge; wisdom is the growth of that self-knowledge through harmonious function according to your inner structure.
- Wisdom is the *process* of applying perception, recording, structure, function to growth - physically, emotionally and spiritually.
- Wisdom is living in conscious, perceptive awareness.
- Wisdom is the balancing of the square of spectrum, semantics, structure, octave in practical, aware, conscious and rhythmic everyday function.

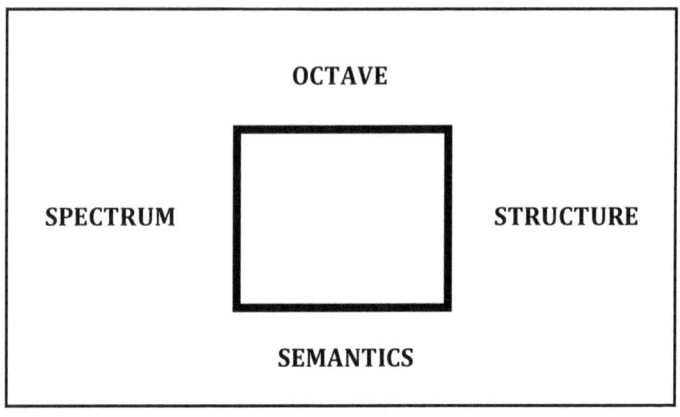

- Wisdom is intelligent preparation for useful everyday living; for integrating balance, awareness and *conscious* growth in everything you say, feel, think and do.

- Wisdom is never permitting yourself to get so lost in any *one* idea or function that you say this is IT - and then become unconscious.

- Wisdom is the intelligent awareness and control of all that you say, feel and do. It is partly a trained skill.

- Wisdom means losing ALL monoideism and blind specialization.

Let us now look at what wisdom is NOT.

Wisdom is **NOT**:

- knowledge
- concepts
- aphorisms
- dogmas

- platitudes
- religion
- philosophy
- science
- words
- ideas
- scripture
- opinions
- tradition
- customs
- habits
- fixed formulation

Wisdom is the end result of a process of integral function - it must be LIVED to be known - experience is the start of wisdom. Wisdom is the child of the true Gnosis; its purpose is to bring eternity into time through true natural order functioning. It can never be completely stated in words; it sparks a true resonance in one's mind-heart between the microcosm (human, the little order) and the macrocosm (the Big Order) in which man is integrated and functions.

Ignorance of humankind's true relation, dependence and correlation with the larger universe deprives humankind of sanity, health, true function, and proper growth in the Galactic Order of Hierarchies which form and maintain and renew untold universes beyond the power of number, image or word to contain.

Wisdom, then, may be referred to as that energy-substance-force from eternity which can enter into us after due preparation; it manifests as function within the Light, Love, Wisdom and Power of True Gnosis.

Wisdom may be termed the non-verbal essence-seed of balanced thinking, feeling, speaking and rest.

It is an experience; it must be experienced in daily life function until its radiant, life-giving and healing power is felt in your bones, belly, head, heart and hand. It is sometimes called the digestion of the Light; it leads to inspired, spontaneous and healthy functioning.

In sum, then, we have the receiver, the wisdom-energy radiation, and their proper ordering and combining to make possible a blending and application in everyday use of the higher forces from the realms of the Noetic Light.

Generally, wisdom and dogmatic speech are in inverse ratio - the more speech the less the wisdom can enter us to dispel the delusionary darkness in our mind.

2

**From Ideas to Structure
Or
From Blindness and Identification to Sanity**

STAR LAUNCH 1

Let your life a shining spiral be
Emblem of Eternity
Coolly train your mind-hand-heart
In the Order of the Cosmos to become a part.

Structure your life, from ideas be free
A conscious worker in Infinity
Not in words, concepts, or thought so blind
But in perception your freedom find.

The daily tasks become a mode
So you can train on freedom's road
Free from compulsive thought and feeling
That sets judgement blind and reeling.

Have NO opinions is the Middle Way
By words and emotions not led astray
Measure your actions with clear, clean sight
And with perception conquer unbalance's fright.

The Law of Three you daily use
So that fear and attachment you soon will lose
Measure consciously each passing thought
So in attachment's net you'll never be caught.

Isidore Friedman

As long as a person is polarized to ideas, and ideas only, he must and will be deluded in every area of his everyday functioning. Since the building blocks of the universe are atoms, then an atom is the first structure and is the base from which all else is constructed.

Now, when we train ourselves to think and operate structurally and functionally, we begin to tread the path of the gods. Words with no stable context, and ideas without structure capable of validation through function, test and experiment, not only breed delusion like a stagnant swamp breeds mosquitoes, but actually weaken and deteriorate our sensory-motor nervous system, making clear perception and understanding impossible.

Insanity may tentatively be defined (in the Natural Order) as:

- Believing that words are the event-structure-function they represent.
- Uncontrolled, disorganized and chaotic speech, feelings, thought and action-reactive and automatic.
- Living in a state of relative unawareness and unconsciousness.

- Trying to function by thinking and past idea-word noise concepts in your mind, instead of clear perception (seeing) from which structural coordinates can be made for sane, balanced and cool action.

- The blind belief in the efficacy of any authority to solve our problems - only proper use of perception and integrated function correlated to the Natural Order can do that.

- The belief that a magical word or statement will immediately solve any problem - in reality, words (unconscious) proliferate, augment and cause problems where very often they do not exist in the Natural Order.

- Holding the delusion that you function like you think. Nothing could be farther from the truth.

- Has as a prime cause trigger reaction to people, events and things caused by identification with words and ideas. Blind reaction to any word, idea or thought-concept not only compounds the problem, but also tends to bestialize our consciousness, blinding our minds to decent, sane and calm solution of our daily problems through ordered coordination and correlation of the structural factors involved.

- ☙ The use of unmeasured and unconscious speech, thought, feeling and action in most of the areas of daily living.

- ☙ The improper use of your energy.

- ☙ Using too much or too little force necessary to perform any needed function. Our present energy crisis is a small harbinger of the greater difficulty and problems yet to be made because of our unawareness of our own unconscious handling of the energies of thought, feeling and action resident in ourselves. This is also a perversion of the God Force given to us by the Higher Forces and must inevitably bring dire consequences to the possibility of decent and sane living geared to life facts in the Natural Order.

- ☙ Is ALLOWING yourself to worry, fear, rave about, and be governed by your unconscious reaction to every day needs and functions.

- ☙ Is forming opinions, judgments and decisions based mostly, or only, on likes and dislikes.

- ☙ Is unconscious identification with your words, ideas, concepts and thoughts.

Sanity grows by gradation (degree) and is a direct function of how aware you can become, how clear your perceptions are (not modified or dirtied or obfuscated by past thoughts, feelings and memories) and how conscious you are or can become of your energy or vibratory impingements.

Sanity, then, is a process of gradually:

- Becoming more conscious and aware of your thoughts, feelings and actions.

- Developing the ability and skill to set up tables of relative importance and learn to sense the relative proportions necessary for Natural Order function.

- Sanity becomes possible when one learns to reason by coordinates; the other kinds of reasoning are delusion breeding, inadequate and tend to breed chaos, frustration and destruction.

- Sanity becomes possible when one learns to apply the law of three to daily function.

- Sanity depends on the ability one may acquire to measure one's thoughts, feelings, actions; to correlate them to a functional and relevant purpose and then to apply them to the daily life calmly.

- Sanity depends on your ability to stay cool and avoid emotional thinking.

- Your sanity varies in direct proportion to your knowledge-application of the Laws of the Natural Order; without some knowledge of these cosmic laws, it is impossible to be sane.

- The constant effort to balance your thought-feeling-action spectrum, and the application of the law of alternation to your life begins to prepare the necessary structures in you to make sanity possible.

- Sanity is perception, thinking and judgment-decision based only. Memory and habit-run patterns from the past can only lead to insanity.
- Sanity is balance, right proportion, rhythmic alternation, co-functional alignment of your thought-feeling-energy spectrum in daily living.
- It is impossible to stay sane in today's world without a good sense of humor.
- De-hypnosis and de-conditioning of past memory habits and thought-feeling-action automatic responses must become established inside you before sanity can even start.
- Sanity cannot be born without controlled, soft, slow and conscious speech; incoherent, unconscious, rapid and uncontrolled speech rapidly generates insanity.
- Sanity becomes impossible today without a large patience. Patience can be defined as a conscious, systematic understanding of what is happening.
- A working knowledge of general semantics is a necessity for sanity, safety and general wellbeing in a manipulative, mad society geared to reacting mouth-noises (words

without a referent and without any stable context to permit a validation as to truth).

Sanity has as one of its first requirements the learning of how to function, evaluate and work by gradation (gradual approximation).

Sanity needs an understanding of process to become functional in everyday life; without this, all the logic, ideas, concepts, dogmas, opinions rotate into chaos and destruction through being against the Natural Order.

A trained attention: choices based on calm and cool perception of basic coordinates; decisions based on measurement and correlation available to amount of resistance to be overcome; constant scanning and review of new factors; conscious and aware thinking derived from clear perception (not from precedent, habit, custom and tradition); detachment from all inhibitions, repressions, and compulsions in the psychic-nature -these are true cosmic tools.

3

The Fallacies of Aphorisms, Platitudes, Ancient Scriptures, Ideas, Traditions and the Past As A Functional Guide To Intelligent Living and Growth In the Here. Now.

Star Fire 10

To be free from emotion's searing heat
In the cool of reason your consciousness seat
Perceive the lie of the uttered word
that prisons and permeates and poisons the herd.

Make attention stronger than symbol
Co-measure the Light, be it much, or a thimble
To fit the seeking, question mind
That has come to you, itself to find.
Strengthen Perception, Attention, Choice
That your true Inner Flame may grow and rejoice
And live, and love, and do and be
A Conscious Light in Eternity.

With Light and Love and Wisdom-Power
Restructure your life hour by hour
See clean, uncolored by word or thought
In automatic concept never caught.

With patient structure your every day
To properly tread the Cosmic Way
A reservoir of light from the cosmic pool
A functional instrument in Infinity's School.

Isidore Friedman

IT IS FREQUENTLY THE CUSTOM TO QUOTE SOME HOARY platitude or aphorism or scripture as authority and precedent for what we should or shouldn't do now. This is then given as a cogent and prescribed course of action.

A solid, scientific and close scrutiny of these sayings and platitudes show them to be, for the most part, structurally inadequate for any kind of intelligent living and functioning in today's world, beside being dangerous, delusion breeding, ignorance-fostering and wrong; many of them being only mouth noises with no referent in reality or the Cosmic process.

Study of the past has value, but, an unconscious worship of the past as the source of all good and proper guide to the new is like the continued study of the mother's womb to learn how to handle the new born baby *after* it has been ejected from the mother. Once the baby has been catapulted into birth in a new and different space-time, it must breathe, eat, digest, eliminate and function for itself - it can no longer take subsistence from the mother's womb physically. Later, psychic independence must be earned and learned, and then the process of individualization must be entered, worked on and developed. Always remember, this is a process - not an idea, or hope, or desire or concept, or saying - it is a process, which means function in an alternating helix spiral that pulsates, grows, eliminates and constantly forms new dynamic balance.

Values developed solely or mostly on the mental or cortical level do not lead to survival. Clichés, catchwords, slogans and propaganda using the words "everyone" or "all humanity" or "always" or "never" are not only semantic gibberish and noise (having no referent in the natural order of the Cosmic Process) but invariably lead to false-to-fact evaluations and manifolds; basing our actions on verbal noises can only lead to chaos, confusion, fear, frustration and all the other manifestations of a disintegrating society shown so crystal clear in the newspapers, movies, and TV screens.

There is also this tremendous automatic pressure on every level of the society to manipulate and force certain ideas and actions which are "good" and for "everyone's" benefit. Being based on ignorance of the natural order process, all these manipulations augment and proliferate the decay and chaos processes.

The blindness of our leaders and politicians who use swindlers algebra constantly, making the symbol seem to be the reality, and using second order abstractions (unconsciously) to force large masses of unconscious people into compulsive, unaware living and buying, sets negative spirals of magnetic field forces into operation whose end result must be insanity.

Let us, then, constantly apply the true measure and guide and protection of the natural order - any time we read, hear, or see something, we ask ourselves, "How well does this correlate with and fit the natural order process and the way it functions?"

If there is structural agreement, we know it is holy (whole) and we may accept with reasonable confidence that the motion of this idea-force into the future is good. If it does not conform to the natural order it should be avoided like the plague.

The higher can only be and grow properly from a sound and structured base in the lower - to raise a tall building without first establishing a sound foundation (which is hidden from sight, usually) is to make chaos, even catastrophe certain in the fairly near future.

Words, ideas, concepts, platitudes, sayings, *all scriptures* of *any kind*, these are useful in a very limited context of historical comparison - in Organics they are always secondary to life facts (structure-function-order of Cosmos). Our thinking-feeling-doing should be firmly based on the experiences of the natural order in everyday function - from this we can grow organically and solidly to an ever brighter, healthier and more joyful future as a beginning conscious co-creator with the Light forces from the Noetic levels.

All verbal constructs from the cortical level have a partly useful but very limited function in the larger growth spectrum of a cosmic Being.

Identification with *any* word-form or verbal statement has an automatic tendency to solidify and trap a person into a frozen symbol, which can then become a prison and stifle the seeker's continuing growth into ever larger concentric circles of usefulness, service and work in the larger cycle of being-becoming which is a process of integrating purposefully into ever larger areas of Cosmic Consciousness.

Humanity's oldest prayer was the prayer for light; in a certain sense, evolution may be regarded as the shining forth of ever greater Light and Beauty through ever more flexible and permeable forms so that a larger cosmic purpose may be implemented in the Here-Now.

True freedom (on a deeper level) can only begin when the person has gradually and scientifically released himself from being possessed by his automatic thought-feeling forms from the past, automatically being triggered in the present, and molding the future into the past because of unconscious reactive actions.

Sanity, from an Organics viewpoint, means becoming oriented to energy-streams, field-forces, ray patterns and beginning to orientate your thinking-feeling-doing to structure rather than ideas - ideal-idols concepts, thoughts and verbal forms.

In Organics, the ATTENTION is helped and made to become stronger than the symbol - then unconsciousness through automatic verbal association may be overcome, and one can mount the step ladder of becoming a clairvoyant (a clear seer), a Christos in bud.

4

Some Prime Factors

STAR LAUNCH 2

Balance is God – to tread the way
From a dark whining clod to a shining ray
To fashion Light with a web of thought
So that heavenly speres in matter are caught.

To pulse with the spheres in synchronized motion
to consciously work in Eternity's ocean
To form in Light's Field a spiral way
In which force and form eternally play.

In Vulcan's forge to fashion the fire
Of Light and Wisdom and Love to inspire
The pulsing spark from the Inner Flame
Which, balanced, must the forces of chaos tame.

And the Crown of Light with patience long
Is set on the head when Wisdom is strong
And the Light, the Wisdom, the Power, all Three
Sing a loving song through Infinity.

And the light energy spirally changes
The Questing Thought through Eternity ranges
And the chorded tones of Builder Rays
Structure and form the cosmic ways.

Isidore Friedman

THE MACROCOSM (GREAT WORLD) AND MICROCOSMOS (human world) are related in structure, octave and spectrum.

In terms of process this relationship is subjectivity; in terms of situation, it is objectivity.

So, process is time; everything is dimension (space); and space is relationship.

Now, there are two basic motions to everything, for this chapter.

Outward

- male-active
- positive
- will
- from center to circumference
- centrifugal

Inward

- female-receptive
- negative
- desire
- from circumference to center
- centripetal

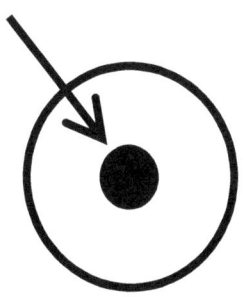

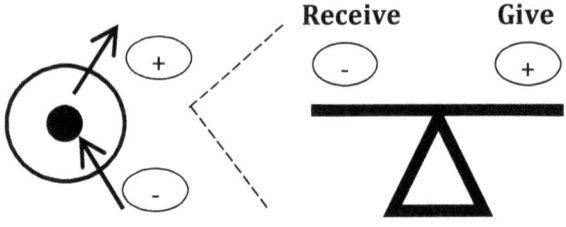

These two motions should be balanced in a third - the conscious awareness of the doer.

The balancing of the outer and inner impulse forces through the application of the law of three; the law of progressive approximation (gradation); the laws of digestion-assimilation-review and elimination.

To even *start* to do these things by:

- first becoming aware of them and their necessity in *every* activity of your daily life.

- application of these balancing principles to every function, every day and everywhere you are is already a *major* step in the right direction. Eventually this must lead to a polarization of the being to the higher light forces - then the seed of a cosmic being changes into a conscious worker.

Now for this measuring and balancing process to take place *properly* in us, we must make it a constant goal to keep cool mentally and emotionally tranquil every day and every hour of the day. This is a *cumulative* skill which has to be built up by the being and in the being gradually, surely, scientifically and *persistently*. In fact, it becomes wise to look upon the daily events as an exercise in calm, cool, ordered and *unemotional* work and response to the day's needs and happenings.

Remember it is *always* and *only* by degrees that we conquer the destructive dragons of old habits and negative actions that ever seek to drag us down in the muddy cesspool of the disordered personality and there destroy us by fragmentization of thought and feeling and the resultant energy loss, which is disastrous. More and more it becomes necessary to remain in perception in a gradually increasing spectrum of time and function.

As often as possible, daily exercises should be done on the practice of perception - of learning to look at something nakedly - without any associations from the past, present or future. This is a practical task and skill whose effects are intensely far-reaching and unexpected. It can only be done by *tiny* degrees and the length of time one can do this usually expands in *tiny* increments; doing this drill forcibly and in a hurry makes it worthless.

Begin also to watch, become very conscious of:

- ❦ when your voice starts to heat up and become higher pitched

- when you speak too fast, too intensely, too positively, too negatively, too *much*
- unconscious and dispersed speech

Begin to tabulate on small file cards all automatic reactions during the day of anything or idea or event that:

- turns you on emotionally unconsciously
- turns you off the same way
- that causes you to worry, fear, doubt
- brings on pictures out of your control
- makes you like or dislike deeply
- plunges you into the past and gets you lost there
- that triggers off hosts of automatic memories, good or bad
- starts a sinking feeling in your stomach
- makes you feel ashamed or guilty
- causes your hands to perspire a lot
- pulls you out of present time awareness - and makes it quite difficult to get back in it again
- very happy, very sad or very moody

Become painfully aware of the terrible unconscious waste of your life energy going on in you.

Begin to apply consciously and conscientiously the principle of least effort in *all* your daily activities.

(Again, in a graduated scale, by degrees). After some time working on plugging up the energy leaks caused by unconscious doing, enough energy will have been accumulated to start sealing the emotional-mental leaks in your vehicles as you go through your daily chores. This will usually be very difficult and discouraging at the beginning. However, it is an absolute necessity if you truly want to rise to, and stabilize in, the higher frequency level called the Noetic plane of function - knowing and seeing and doing by direct perception of the Cosmic Process - not by thinking or comparing or jiggling of associative circuits in the brain.

It is vital that a maximum energy arise in you so that this growth to the higher can have sufficient energy drive to happen.

Next, you must begin to apply the principle of *thorough digestion* of your daily experiences *consciously*. The calamity going on in most of the younger people's lives today is, to a very great extent, caused and aggravated by laying more unconscious experiences on top of the completely undigested experiences inside their subconscious minds. Undigested experiences create deadly poisons in the mind, body and nervous system precisely the same as undigested food creates poisons in the blood and body which hamper and eventually destroy function, and then life.

Some time should be taken every day, preferably in the early evening, and this procedure followed:

- First, breathe deeply, softly, slowly and rhythmically for about two minutes.
- Relax, yawn, blink eyes, stretch.
- Then, *very calmly* run the day's events *backwards* in your mind, just as a movie camera might run a film from end to its beginning.
- Tabulate on a large file card (dated) all the times during the day when:
    - you became unconscious through automatic speech, emotions and actions.
    - you violated the *basic* rule of Organics of m.y.o.b. (mind your own business) through an unconscious upsurge of sympathy for something that welled up in you.
    - you talked
        - too much
        - too fast
        - too excitedly
        - too unconsciously
        - identified with what you were saying-seeing-hearing-feeling
    - lost, partially or completely, your sense and awareness of present time in the Here-Now and literally reverted to the past (or future) *unconsciously*.
    - actually try to see the life energy being poured out of you and *wasted*, just like a leaky gas tank will empty itself and stop the car long before the necessary destination is reached.

You must practice, practice, practice non-reactivity to other people's words, ideas, advice, counsel, solicitation, anger, disgust, admonitions, etc., etc., etc. Otherwise, you get pulled off your *own* center (your God within) and get sucked into a diabolical vortex of undigested, disordered, foul and poisonous energies emanating from disordered, unhappy, unbalanced and disoriented people. Then you die, for all practical work purposes.

It is axiomatic in Organics that negatively polarized, mentally disordered and emotionally polarized people *must automatically* manifest, reflect, augment, and create hate, fear, frustration, anger, jealousy, resentment, irritation and give destructive advice and suggestions on *EVERY-THING* - they can't help doing so – it's their state of being - just as ice reflects cold, and steam reflects heat.

A massive, powerful, enduring and centered strength must be *gradually* built up inside your being to enable you to sustain these energy distortions, and not allow them to distort and pull you out of your cosmic orbit and function as a patterner of ordered light and an apprentice to the higher creative forces, helping them to create ordered centers of light through which the cosmic structure-plan may be made manifest.

It is urgent to learn the techniques of skilled and balanced functioning so that prevalent negative and destructive forces rampant in today's society will be unable to destroy you.

To be *deeply* affected by other people's likes and dislikes and compulsive thoughts-feelings-actions is to stare into the face of total insanity.

To want, or need, or hunger for other people's approval; to be deeply moved by other people's disapproval is to enter complete chaos; remembering always that you remain *conscious*.

An ordered and aware consciousness is the doorway to heaven; a disordered and reactive and unaware consciousness is already hell itself and the path to misery, frustration, disease and increasing chaos.

Birth into light is impossible without a long struggle with the darkness of ignorance, both within and without the seeker.

Reflection, refraction are not only physical phenomena, they also have their exact mental counterparts.

Newton's three laws of motion apply equally well to mental phenomena as well as physical.

Patience is the road to the gods; a being's true stature is in direct proportion to the amount of intelligent patience he manifests.

After all is said and done - there is much being said and practically nothing done. Delusion quickly enters the mouth of a glib talker.

5

**The Importance of General Semantics;
Without It, Occultism Degenerates
Into the Manipulating and Proliferating of
Symbols Without Any Referents In
Reality (Cosmic Process).**

STAR LAUNCH 30

The battle of words closes mind's true eye
Their insane gibberish makes reason to die
Without reason, the beast awakens emotion's heat
And Love and Sanity and Wisdom retreat.

And words have become a mindless hammer
To distort and manipulate crowd's bestial yammer
And frustrate every decent goal
Words without referents have no body or soul.

And this word-bred delusion poisons every relation
And steadily decays the entire nation
And the confusion mounts from bad to worse
And violence and hatred every level do curse.

And misevaluated words bring untold confusion
As the lies of the words daily create illusion
More chaos and destruction they hourly release
Which push further away any chance of peace.

And the animal greed just grows and grows
From every side verbal poison flows
And the hostile forces all insensate
Our gradual destruction subtly create.

Isidore Friedman

IN THE CORTICAL FUNCTION, THE USE OF SPEECH AND writing, the use of any and all verbal images, these are the functions of the intellect, a word machine. Inherently, the intellect can create nothing, but it can categorize and label and compare and make neat little idea-verbal packages which are useful, providing we sharply recognize its function and application, and also its limitations.

The verbal intellect, by its very nature, *must* dip into the past every time we use a word - hence it may be classed as a subconscious computer.

We are stringently warned by Korzybski on the vital difference between intentional (word) orientation and extensional (process, life-fact) orientation.

In the former, we focus attention on words, ideas, concepts, etc., etc., language-forms, "meaning" of words (which have no existence in Reality). Through the steady use of unconscious abstractions we become lost in a vast, roaring, chaotic fog and jungle of verbal clichés and associations having nothing to do with energy and Reality (Cosmic Process). We then *evaluate* on chimeras and meaningless noises, and try to function therein, commit verbal murder, destroying both ourselves and others in a barrage of meaningless noises and sounds divorced from life-facts; a total waste of life energy.

In the latter, we slowly, surely and persistently, by *degrees*, re-focus our orientation to structure-function order of the cosmos, gradually learning to function and be guided by life-facts and structures.

We deliberately practice and learn how to structure our language to conform to, as much as possible, the natural order of the Universe. Instead of floating in a miasma of unrelated ideas, we learn to structure our thinking and acting, *slowly*, in line with how things actually work in and through patterned energy in patterns of interweaving relationships - saving us endless energy which is usually lost in frantic, compulsive, heating and useless speech.

We carefully learn to use TIME properly; we persistently train and re-train our minds to function in process-thinking, thus paying proper attention to structure-function-order, and phase, pattern and cycle - intentional orientation (word-idea meaning focus) is gradually replaced by extensional (function) orientation, and we gradually work out of the quagmire-muck shadow-word noises and idea-opinions-thought dogmas into the solid, satisfying, dependable and sane safety of structural functioning and operational descriptions, free from dogma, doubt, fanaticism and verbal fisticuffs indulged in constantly because we all have different associations for the same word; the confusion can only become more confused in this way.

There is no truth in words alone; there is no sanity in words alone; there is no natural order correlation in words alone; there is no *answer* to any deep problem through words alone; there is no satisfying relations between people through words alone; there is no heart nourishment and sharing of inner essences through words alone - all that words, divorced from a stable context and without validation of meaning, can do is increase the ignorance, darkness, fear, worry and chaos which is already too prevalent.

All verbal knowledge has no direct relationship with whatever Reality is; and words, by their very nature, and our ignorance of their limitations, are essentially misleading.

Words that are structurally orientated to nature processes and functions; words that come deep from the core of LIVING experiences; words that are specifically geared to describing and detailing energy patterns; words that are simple, sharp, direct, and succinct - words that nearly always have a referent in Reality - these lead to sanity, hope, and an expanding and useful life, and fulfillment in work. Otherwise, delusion grows.

In summation, then:

- Work towards extensional orientation.
- Use a referent for every important word used.
- Do not get lost in exhortations and emotionally polarized statements.

- Do not become hypnotized by your own brilliant rhetoric.
- Never lose the vital application of the law of three.

6

Becoming Conscious

STAR FIRE 15

A point, a line, a circle-bound
A light field is formed, spins round and round
The alternate pulse of a magnetic ray
Sets structure and function for a cosmic play.

A vortex, deep, in matter asleep
Spirals its mighty field
Carves out by light the chaos-night
And forms a patterned yield.

That pulsates now, a beginning force
Through endless cycles, to return to its source
A mighty star of glowing light
To join warrior aeons in the cosmic fight.

That Light and Love, and Wisdom-Power
Through the music of sound, create a galaxy flower
To sing its chord of flux in rhyme
In its ordered growth from the cosmic slime.

And the Lords of Order, through pattern and force
Cleanse the forming fields of chaos-dross
Adding another form and line
True cosmic story to properly refine.

Isidore Friedman

PART OF BECOMING CONSCIOUS, OF LIVING IN A state of perceptive cognition; of being an actual seer (see-er) in everyday life, is like a skill that has to be acquired through conscious, every day, intentional practice, like learning to play a musical instrument or to drive a car well.

In simpler words, it is, in part, a function which is earned and acquired by *degrees*, in *small gradational steps*. Now, doing the conscious drills every day, no matter how you feel, or how discouraged you may get; mustering the strength and awareness *not* to be sucked in and controlled by your unconscious thoughts and feelings, keeping everlastingly at it *must*, sooner or later, free you and set you on the next step of living and doing more consciously.

The skill grows by almost imperceptible degrees; however, proof that you are heading in a correct direction and growing towards seership will manifest as:

- a diminishing of emotional thinking.
- a feeling of the inadequacy and futility of unconscious talk in improving or settling any problem.

- ❦ a gradual strengthening of your attention and awareness to become stronger than any symbol, verbal or written.
- ❦ a refusal, complete and unequivocal, to become mentally or emotionally upset or excited by anything that is said, seen or heard in the outer world.
- ❦ a cessation of the unconscious use of clichés and platitudes in your everyday speech and conversations.
- ❦ the regulating control and diminishing of *emotional force* used in your speaking every day.

It is absolutely vital to stop giving unconscious advice to anyone at the drop of a hat. Unless you are really together and integrated, your compulsive and impulsive advice will probably be resented or misunderstood, or applied wrongly, thus causing more harm than good. So, for a very long time in your growth into conscious awareness, so far as advice is concerned: JUST DON'T.

Also, the wasted force, time and thought could much better be employed elsewhere.

Now, one of the very interesting things that begins to happen after a while, is that as you begin to get more conscious, you concomitantly begin to see, hear and understand more. Problems that were not really problems - that were just caused by an unconscious and ignorant functioning - begin to dissolve into thin air.

Too much force in your thinking and feeling distorts the reception and balancing of the signals to you from the environment through the nervous system.

There is a disease which we can call *neuro-americanitis*, which is the remaining in a perpetual state of nervous excitement, itchy-twitchy in our responses to the environment, in a perpetual and excited state to go places, see things, argue over anything, and attract attention.

This then makes for superficial and inadequate responses in everything - until this is slowed down, it is physically and psychologically impossible to function in an easy, relaxed yet adequate way.

This constant drainage of our life energies makes it literally impossible to perceive anything properly; wrong perception means wrong evaluation and action.

This monkey-like jumping of the mind; this constant flickering and unconscious reaction of the attention; some negative happening outside that automatically triggers off uncontrolled torrents of emotions, thoughts, actions; this constant false need to be continually stimulated by different sensations; this tremendous unconscious waste of life-energy in emotional thinking and Niagara of speech - all this and more wrong function in most of what we do - so deplete our life force that:

- ❦ there is no energy left to protect yourself from the negative vibrations in the environment.
- ❦ there is no energy left to power your drive to accomplish whatever life purpose or goal you may want.

One of the greatest lacks today, by and large, is the lack of a sense of relative importance, or relative proportion. Thus, the vital reasoning by co-ordinates can't be done.

It is also vitally necessary to so increase your sense of repose and poise that nothing from the outside can push or pull you off your calm center. This can and must be strengthened daily and hourly, gradually so increasing your insulation that the power of the outer to affect you will gradually become less and less; more attention, energy, will and time will be left for you to accomplish your true work in life. You will also thus be protected from the negative.

Slowly, carefully, persistently, like a gigantic, slow-moving, but powerful turtle, refuse to resonate with the little chaos-storms in your everyday function. Stop emphasizing and paying attention to trifles in events and the trivia that most people seem riveted on, to the complete loss of perceptive awareness and balanced living. Be in control and direction of your attention. It's your most basic and important protection.

In the ancient books of integration, there were certain basic factors that, like a constantly recurring musical theme, were woven into the workers' daily life:

1. Basic persistent training was given in clear, sharp, powerful and calm thought.

2. Actions were integrated and synthesized using the measure of the triune God, the Law of Three.

3. Speech that was low, soft, slow, calm, measured to the present coordinates of function precisely was skillfully developed.

Very often confused thought and agitated feeling inside can be greatly helped merely by *slowing* the speech, consciously, and of course, lowering and softening the tone. The brittle sound of tense, unconscious, disturbed and emotion-driven speech not only damages the nerves of both speaker and listener, but arouses unconscious resentment and resistance in the listener's mind to what is being said.

Not to mention the automatic tuning in to a highly dangerous spectrum of speech-thought on the inner planes, and so becoming resonated to ever more disturbance, anger and confusion.

The direction, quality and focus of your thought are all important in steering your boat away from the rocks of unconscious living into the safe harbor of balanced living and sane speech.

It is wise to develop a reverse mechanism strongly in you: the hotter and more confused things and events become on the outside, the cooler and more self-ordered must you become on the inside. Again, developed by degrees.

In all things, study, learn, and apply the laws of the Natural Order (structure of Cosmos) which are essentially ordered energy matrices in patterns of relationship.

To be unrelated is to be confused, frightened, doubtful and more dead than alive.

To be related unconsciously is to receive a constant barrage of poor point-events banging at you daily, the boomerang created by your unconsciousness.

Awareness is a skill that can be developed and enlarged by study, application and very persistent practice in daily life.

A very important work triangle that can be applied to any worthwhile goal linking the two worlds.

If it be that man is a biological transducer (both a radio transmitter and a radio receiver in one form), then his entire future depends on his becoming conscious of what he is receiving; and also what he is transmitting. If a man, in his ignorance, is unaware both of what he is receiving, and what he is transmitting; if he is unaware that he is a living electromagnetic field capable of generating and distributing untold billions of frequencies, both destructive and constructive; if he is completely unaware of the fields of force that he is continually emanating; then, by and large, the automatic broadcasting and re-amplification of the negative forces humankind is emanating, because of ignorance of his negative polarization, can destroy civilization in a short while.

Organics was designed and structured to help build a *functional* bridge connecting the different inter-dimensional levels of Being-Becoming.

It is of great importance that the student recognizes the importance of the physical plane as a locus of operations; the Eastern disciplines, for the most part, negate the physical planes in favor of "merging with the All, dewdrop slips into the shining sea, etc., etc." This is *exceedingly* dangerous for the Western seeker, as the physical must be balanced, related, and then used as a base and springboard for exploring the other dimensions through a being-doing, and *never* through either being alone, or doing divorced from a centered stance in being.

A vacuous meditation, and trying to find reality based on ideas and exclusion of the physical base is non-functional - the physical being the ground for the Cosmic Forces.

The most important and exceedingly difficult task for the beginner on the way of integration is to build, develop, strengthen and extend a living sense of synthesis in all that he does - the use of analysis only, not only fragmentizes one's growth, but actually is a reductive process - one loses energy continually, and also the joy of whole functioning, where synthesis is not made an active and useful fulcrum and tool in all activities daily.

Until a person has worked through, understood and dissolved automatic identification with words, his thoughts and feelings, and his concepts (identified with first, second and third order abstractions unconsciously) his deeper inner progress is completely blocked - he turns into some kind of deranged and automatic symbol-machine spouter, and loses *all* contact with functional reality.

To try to live beyond what we know is dangerous. Not to live up to what we know is equally perilous.

Realization results from discipline.

There are many metaphysicians who can look a fact in the face and then deny it with a series of affirmations.

When a small mind takes hold of a big idea, chaos is inevitable.

Do not permit yourself the extravagance of any useless expenditure of energy.

From the past, we inherit a vast jungle of useless, inadequate, energy-wasting and anti-natural order thoughts, feelings, traditions and chaos. The first step is to become aware of this rotting, ignorance breeding and unconscious swamp-of-the-past in us, and then to cleanse it slowly, by degrees, by persistent, small daily efforts, in awareness. This, in alchemy, has been called purification.

Reality can never be obtained through *any* idea, verbal form, concept or word formulation.

It also can never be tasted by only observation - there must be a functional and relevant participation in the higher cosmic electromagnetic (Noetic) fields, which then, by resonance and induction, help awaken and sustain the deeper cosmic energies latent in the being.

There is a basic formula in simple physics which is entirely relevant to the birth and development of the higher awareness in us: energy output is equal to energy input *minus* the loss due to resistance.

Speech and higher realization are not only in inverse proportions but much speech makes higher realization impossible through leakage and waste of life energy.

Unconscious speech and unaware action inevitably create a destructive-frustrating focus of forces; then suck one right into this negative vortex-force inexorably.

To kill time regularly also means to destroy any possibility for the manifestation of your true dreams, needs, functions and vocation.

Well-meaning advice from people who are ignorant and not together is most often not only inadequate and wrong, but if taken seriously, invariably leads to chaos, catastrophe and frustration enveloping the life of the person foolish enough to act on this "advice."

Generalization on anything without a structural knowledge of the context of situation of that thing, is invariably a swamp quicksand into which tumble and die all those who accept the generalization blindly and without deep thought.

Authority based only on the past tradition and old scriptures, without a knowledge of, and testing through structure and function in daily life, is demoniacal, destructive, slave-making and heart breaking - it is the blind leading the blind - until self-destruction through ignorance of the natural order invariably takes place.

Steady, persistent and sharp training is needed to extricate one from the false mirage of words into the tangible energy worlds of structure and function which constitutes our true reality.

It is rarely apparent how unconsciously we use words, without understanding the vital necessity both for a referent for every important word, and for a proper context which actually gives the word its meaning. Any word without a context has absolutely no coherent or functional meaning of any kind - and, its power for delusion and catastrophic, chaos-forming action is literally incalculable.

It should be continuously repeated, hundreds of times if necessary, that the use of words without shared, common experiences to form the living referent, invariably generates misunderstanding, unconsciousness, improper, false-to-fact thinking, feeling and doing and is in essence, completely anti-natural order.

We hide behind the dictionary definition of a word, much like an ostrich buries its head in the sand at the onset of any danger - with equally dangerous results.

As of now, we are all in a very grave danger of both generating insanity and chaos because of our normal ignorance of the true uses of words.

Basically, knowledge may be broken down into two categories:

A) essential knowledge

B) decorative knowledge

Essential knowledge has to do with the structure-function-order of life and the universe. It is extensionally oriented (to life facts) and is *created consciously*.

Decorative knowledge seems to be just a wild proliferation of tradition-habit untested theories, ideas, words, concepts, opinions, dogmas and *unproved* principles which complicate and confuse everything; it then turns into a mire of quicksand, and, because of unconscious intentional (word) orientation and identification with verbal noises, drowns us, sooner or later, slowly or quickly, but *inevitably*. People who take words for things become destructive and dangerously insane.

When a person uses language unconsciously in important situations, he is dropping a time bomb into both his and other peoples' minds which then can explode at any time in the future with very damaging results to either the speaker, his audience or both.

Learning the proper use (function) of words and language is a strict discipline requiring a minimum of at least two or three years of study, application, reflection and daily work – the "normal" use of words in all our media and daily life automatically creates fear, frustration, confusion, hate, misinterpretation, therefore misunderstanding and a host of other negative forces too numerous to tabulate here. A 21st century technology with minds from 2000 B.C. creates a very perilous world to live in.

In previous times, there was not in existence the large aggregates of people herded so closely together that wrong communications could literally destroy millions - rumor is treated as fact.

Unconsciously used words generate all kinds of emotions and thoughts in us; this makes some kind of a nebulous fog inside our head; we then are immersed in this fog, our fears and doubts amplify; we then conclude that the "outside" is this fear-fog in us, and we act from this evaluation. This, of course, is the anatomy of insanity - something like taking a TV set apart to find out where the picture is coming from.

From this miasma-in-our-head, we automatically tune, by resonance, into other people's fog-heads and our present chaos-run society is the almost automatic result.

To become more and more aware, daily, by *degrees*; to train and develop our attention into becoming stronger than any symbol, sight or sound - this is the way out of the quagmire-stench of this ignorance and identification.

All words are abstractions; they have *no direct relationship* with whatever reality is; they are *essentially* misleading. It is very important that the seeker after the Gnosis see cleanly and clearly into words and their use in different orders of abstractions - otherwise identification with word-noises, thoughts, ideas, concepts and opinions takes place automatically and immediately. Once identification has occurred, all further growth into the patterned light is effectively stopped. Idols and ideals-words are set up in the seeker's mind; he then becomes a slave and victim to the thought-forms which he himself has unconsciously created, or accepts the delusions of others.

To argue, become heated or upset, waste energy, to try to force your verbal form onto anyone, even for the best reasons in the world - these are the beginning tracks to insanity, unconsciousness and spiritual death.

Because we have been drenched in words since our birth; because we are constantly bombarded with words and speech every moment of the day; because words become a conditioned hypnosis inside us;

much time and hard, intelligent effort should be made to break from the prison word thoughts which keep our brains in chains.

It is positively a humiliating experience to note in us the continual automatic response to written and spoken word-noises from the outside. The bitter realization that you have no decent, functional referent for well over 90% of the words you hear and use is both a bitter but healthy and awakening shock.

Anyone in this "culture" who does not have a good basic understanding of general semantics must automatically be a victim of and slave to most of the manipulations in news media, business, religion and education.

THE WISDOM BOOK

PART II

STAR FIRE 7: INVOCATION

Let me be as a candle flame
Burning on a windless plane
That my light, though small in the dark
Shall bring to lost seekers a guiding spark.

Cleanse thou me, O Noetic Fire
Of the verbal muck and the race-mind mire
That my Essence, clear and free
Be a guide post to Eternity.

The monkey chatter of the boiling mind
Cool and stop, so that I can find
The golden thread, the frequency form
That structures the way to Infinity's norm.

Protect me from poisoned and obsessing emotions
That tear and destroy like chaos-whipped oceans
Insulate me from the verbal pap
That strengthens the hold of our every-day trap.

From images' delusion protect my heart
That the true Gnosis can soundly start
The process of Wisdom's cleansing power
to build the instrument and structure the hour.

Isidore Friedman

IN SOME OF THE OLDER ALCHEMICAL BOOKS, ALCHEMY was described as a process consisting of several phases:

I. *Putreficatio* - rottingness (rotten), end, decayed, foul, smelly, etc.

II. *Purgatorio* - purging or the beginning of a cleansing process in hell.

III. *Purificatio* - the slow, persistent, steady work of removing and changing the decay in purgatorio into a healthier condition.

IV. *Regeneratio* - the goal of the alchemical process - the birth or rebirth into the new.

Now, each of these processes has a certain time cycle to accomplish its purpose - well over 90% of those who are lured or hypnotized or drift into "yoga," "magic," "mysticism," "occult," "Wicca," etc., haven't the slightest notion of what the process of transmutation or rebirth means, and the necessary steps towards its accomplishment in one's self.

Most often, regeneratio is tried, without the necessary preparatory phases, especially purificatio being entered upon. The effect of this lack is most often disastrous - as this part of the process is the longest, most arduous, painful and difficult of all. All true processes in nature follow a natural-order sequence that is inviolable - the egg is laid, the chick breaks through and is born - and a whole new life commences, different completely from when the chick as yet was inside the shell.

Similarly, if true transmutation and rebirth into a higher being are desired, the order and stages are fixed and inevitable - if not followed in proper phasic and sequential order, the entire process aborts, with some very nasty consequences, to say the least.

There is no short cut to true transmutation and regeneration; each phase must be entered consciously, worked through with an ever-increasing awareness, eaten and digested, its waste eliminated - then the next phase entered, etc., repeat.

The idea of an easy way or entrance to the alchemy of an integrated and balanced life is a product of our sick, decaying and dying "culture" in the heavy throes of putreficatio (self-destruction) and the necessary following stage of purgatorio.

A steady cleansing, training and developing of all our faculties and functions; a thorough disgust at being the slave of our lower animal propensities; a persistent and all-encompassing search for understanding and applying intelligently the laws of the natural order as shown in the structure-function-order of the Cosmos - these will begin the process of transmutation, whose end is birth and establishment into the stage of function on the Noetic level - the Christos made manifest in a form-of-flesh.

It's all a matter of frequencies - function on the lower frequencies (hate, fear, anger, worry, etc.) is hell - the higher frequency of peace, love, wisdom, etc. is heaven.

It is vital at the beginning to comprehend something of the law of progressive approximation (function and growth by degrees) as we live in a scalar universe where everything is in a process of change - a constant oscillation-pulsation pumping life and vitality into everything which then enters the cycle of birth, growth, decay, death and rebirth continually.

Alternation is heaven's first law; God in some of the ancient teachings was often called the Great Pulsator or Great Alternator.

From this very basic insight, it now becomes necessary to *gradually* apply this law of alternation-pulsation to everything we do - to *every* activity in our daily lives, slowly, gradually but persistently.

If we endure and persist long enough, (and it is hard) a different rhythm, in very tiny increments starts to manifest in our everyday lives.

Awareness and persistence in practicing staying in the perceptive state are all very important here.

Perceptive cognition, like everything else in nature, seems to be gained in degrees - something like a weightlifter practices lifting progressively heavier dumbbells. It is exceedingly important to practice sustaining the perceptive attention, by small degrees, for longer and longer periods of time. Eventually it will become your home and resting place (perception) which then matures into the practice of the presence of God in you.

Ordinary thinking, feeling and doing are almost completely automatic replica echoes of the past; being caught up in your own thought-emotion-action closet is like living in an inch - it becomes awfully cramped and uncomfortable and finally unbearable.

Attention is like a muscle that has to be strengthened by constant exercise.

Learning to control and direct your attention and speech is of the essence if you want to build a saner and better life.

Life's energies most often flow to where you place your attention and speech. You should carefully train yourself, day by day and hour by hour, to speak from a focused awareness of the law of three. Gradually, tiny degree by tiny degree, you teach yourself to become more conscious and so to speak and act more consciously. Slowly, impulsive and compulsive speech begins to get weaker and weaker in you - eventually they die, and the portal of heaven (balanced living and a poised mind) opens to your astonished eyes.

Always try to remember that, for now, transmutation and the higher life are both powerful processes - processes always take time, each phase having its own rhythm cycle, which, when combined, assure you of success in whatever creative project or goal you require.

You must train yourself *meticulously* in the practice of being aware of what you are thinking, feeling, doing and saying. Unconsciousness to any degree in these four factors means so many degrees of death have entered and by that much diminished your awareness and your life.

It is intensely difficult, after a lifetime of living among unconscious and innerly dead people, to change, but, there is no other way out of the quicksand of unconscious living than through awareness, conscious effort and directed attention focused on daily functioning.

Always remember that success in any large enterprise comes usually by small degrees - persistent application of attention, choice, conscious thought and decision will build a solid ladder for you to explore the vast fields of eternity.

Do not get stuck on any *one* idea or process - this stops all synthesis-growth instantly.

Unconscious speech, profuse, over-enthusiastic, actually creates an abyss into which it will drag you, sooner or later.

The amount of energy completely wasted in automatic thinking, feeling, and speaking is literally unbelievable. To start to conserve this wasted energy is almost the first step to an integrated new life.

Monitor your speech, emotions, feelings, thoughts - begin to observe how automatic they are, and how *very little* of your functions are under your control.

Next, gradually but firmly pull your attention and energy and focus out of as many senseless and wasted activities that you can.

Do you talk too much? Too fast? Too intensely? Too diffusely? Too positively? Too unconsciously? Too compulsively? Too urgently? With too much force? Too pompously? Too arrogantly? Etc., etc., etc. Then do something about it.

Rhythm, measured motion, is one of the great master keys in living a creative and useful life - though difficult, a measured rhythm of some kind must be established in your daily life - this alternation-pulsation change in your life will pump new energy, insights and life into your daily function as nothing else can. Try to alternate your activities as much as possible - thus you begin to approach a true and basic natural order function in your life.

Now, after some of this rhythmic alternation has become a part of your daily life function, try by *very small degrees*, to stop thinking and focus your attention-energies onto perceiving - pick any common object (a knife, fork, pencil, cup, book, etc.) and place it on the table about 12 – 15 inches away from you. Then try to look at it without any associations (thought, feelings, ideas, etc., etc.)

On the average, this will be very difficult to do. However, work at it gradually, lengthening the time in which you can look at an object clearly - without any associational thought, image, word, idea or concept from the "past" impinging on the screen of your attention.

By small, progressive degrees, lengthen the time you can thus remain in perception without thoughts.

Then, throughout the entire day, begin to turn off the automatic association machinery that triggers on in so many of your daily activities. This, by the way, will give you more energy to deal with things properly, since less will be wasted in unconscious cerebration, speech, and action.

Become a miser - hoard your energy as if it were the most precious thing in your life. (It is.) For all practical purposes it is God and the way to God - your bridge to infinity.

Watch for unconscious stiffening and tensions in your face, jaws, back of neck, arms and legs - loosen them continually till it becomes natural for you and your body to be in a loose, relaxed state most, if not all, of the time.

It is impossible for any of your functions to go well if there is automatic tension in any of your organs.

Don't eat too fast; don't try to do tomorrow's work today; do well and intelligently what has to be done *now*; make some intelligent, unhurried preparation for what has to be done in the immediate future, then rest in peaceful and profound perception calmly, like a duck floating on the surface of a still pond.

Do not allow any person, place, thing or circumstance to rob you of your poise in the center - if you have to leave center for any reason, return back immediately when you can.

Watch for *any* rising heat in your voice; this is a pretty precise barometer indicating that you are losing your center and opening the door for a mare's nest of chaos to clobber you mercilessly.

Restrict your speech *only* to necessary discussion - refuse to take the bait and argue over *anything*; do whatever has to be done as effortlessly and cleanly as possible.

You are to train your mind to focus more and more on the present; constant complaint about the past and constant fear of the future turn life into a veritable hell of negative emotion and wasted speech.

Enjoy your daily, necessary contacts; be constantly aware of whatever is going on around you in this living moment.

Try not to talk about your problems, hopes and fears to every Tom, Dick and Harry you meet - seek to know all, but yourself remain unknown.

Train your mind:

- ❦ not to respond to trivia.

- not to waste attention on unnecessary theories, concepts, ideas, opinions, ideals and verbal gymnastics not having to do with your daily, immediate functional needs.
- not to generate a vast jungle of interesting mouth-noises without a referent in the living reality which is our Father-Mother Creator, Nature.
- not to bother about what most people (especially those around you) are doing or not doing.
- not to agree *or* disagree automatically with what is heard or thought of around you.
- to prefer intelligent failure from which you learn and grow strong, rather than success gained from the behests of another blindly.

It is very wise to:

- not to be too profoundly depressed at failure.
- not be too blindly happy at success.

This mental equilibrium will help keep you sane.

Structurally speaking it is essential:

- to strengthen, deepen, widen, direct and control your attention as one of your most basic tools to carve out a life suited to your structure and coordinates.
- to be aware that the untrained and undisciplined attention becomes a fertile

breeding ground for all the chaos and insanity generated by people in these rapidly changing times.

- to spend some time *every day* in training and exercising your attention so that you may at will place it anywhere necessary, and remove it calmly - an attention that is not under control brings disorder, illness and frustration into our lives automatically.

- to be aware that one of the important factors in true thinking is *directed* attention - this is both a capacity and a skill which, by intelligent work, can be increased tenfold, bringing so much more ease and ability for better function in your life.

Development, control, direction and *application* of our attention, choice and decision must be gradually built up inside you - otherwise, a sane, creative, integrated and happy life becomes impossible.

Hoard your energy like a miser; do not waste even a drop on negative, useless, automatic and hypnotized thoughts, feelings, actions, concepts, words, ideas and emotions. You should slowly prune away these unnecessary blights on your tree of life so that it may bear wisdom's fruits to nourish those lost in the outer jungle of identifications, words, ideas and fragmented concepts and functions.

De-hypnosis and de-conditioning from past events, words, ideas and speech are both exceedingly painful and difficult, and, at the same time, an urgent and desperate necessity if real growth of the being into the Gnosis is desired. You must die to the past to be born again.

Control and direction of your energy in all *daily life functions* are as necessary as control and direction of your steering wheel when driving your car at very high speeds. To let anyone else control and direct your life energy is to enter the land of the slaves and become a robot set into motion automatically by clever words, ideas and directives from an almost completely chaotic and destructively-polarized "culture."

The basic first steps out of unconsciousness and automatic reaction into a growing awareness and conscious function are relatively simple, but exceedingly difficult to practice in everyday life because of the tremendous outer vortex of sensation-stimuli, and outer hypnotic focus.

As long as the seeker's consciousness (unconsciousness more likely) is focused on his emotions - as long as he is tightly glued to reacting, robot-wise to his likes-dislikes - the way to the higher perception is tightly closed.

The true way can only be trod by an individual; at least, by one who is *starting* to think for himself, gradually freeing himself from the blinding fetters of authority, custom, habit, precedent and lazy thinking, as well as his *own* negative emotions and actions.

Emotional reaction to, or, recognition of, the statement of a verbal "truth," is really light-years away from a functional understanding of what the statement may be the symbol for, or its referent.

After all is said and done, the ratio of what is said to what is DONE is at least a billion to one.

It is so extremely easy to talk, to get carried away by words, stirred emotions and idea-thoughts, to become thus completely deluded as to life-facts (structure-function, order of Cosmos, God).

Any and all actions then, based on these emotional verbal-delusions, leads to anti-natural order actions; this then inexorably leads to chaos and destruction.

One of the saddest and most dangerous effects of unconscious, compulsive talking-emotionism, is the tremendous waste of life energy that thus takes place. Since energy is the direct bridge to the higher levels of being-doing-meaning, no energy inexorably means stasis, rotting in the muck-quicksand of the lower levels of the race psyche, a complete slave and victim to unconscious identification which eat and waste all your energy, leaving no energy to surmount and gradually work out of the old race psyche. This is a living death.

In summary, then, you must forge the tools by means of which you can tunnel your way through and out of the thick miasma of fears, worries, hatred, separating delusion and ignorance called the old race psyche. For this you need to understand, control, direct and purify (chemically speaking) your tools:

- ❦ thoughts and concepts
- ❦ your emotions, likes and dislikes
- ❦ your automatic compulsive and impulsive actions
- ❦ your discursive, automatic and pointless speech.

You must train yourself, hour by hour and day by day, to remain relatively calm in the midst of the emotional commotion, heat and tremendous pressures generated by living in a more or less unsane and unconscious society.

The daily, hour by hour, training of your mind in attention without tension; in meeting the day's events with focused relaxation; in learning visualization without fixation - bit by bit, by degrees, the tools of your consciousness will be assembled, tempered by life, and applied to daily living - you will begin to shed the old attitudes and reactions; a larger, more impersonal view will enter your being and you will grow in understanding and life-wisdom through intelligent faith, love and effort.

On the level of manifestations, *everything is relative* - there are no absolutes in any field of endeavor. Now, if we apply an absolute standard (verbal or otherwise) to a relative situation, we are making for serious trouble.

Perception and thinking; perception and speaking - these are all in inverse ratio. The more thinking, the less the perception. The more speaking, the less the perception.

It is an interesting experiment to either diminish or stop the thinking-speaking for a few days. The differences in the perceptive levels will be remarkably changed for the better.

Action done from a fragmented consciousness must become fragmented actions. There is no magic to this, only direct perception of what is.

You must begin to weed out all the unconscious reactions you have in the physical world - and *persist* in so doing until you have cleansed your being and aura of some of the poisoned, limited, automatic associations of the memory. Your attention *must*, gradually, become stronger than all symbols - verbal, emotional, mental, physical, etc. - otherwise, the delusions can never cease.

It is finally the set focus, the tuned, toned and trained direction of the cosmic forces within one that truly matter.

A sure sense of synthesis is one of the pearls of great price. It is impossible to perceive and judge anything outside of its natural order context - in fact, one definition of meaning is that it's the relationship of a part to a larger whole.

Basic meaning in any thing is a triadic blend relationship including the this, the that, and the *interval* between.

Structure, function, order, relationship, pattern, meaning, energy, synthesis, love, alternation - these are all infinite-valued words, multi-ordinal words which can be hooked up into endless contexts and provide endless insights providing the function of words is thoroughly understood.

Repressed needs, when overcome, tend to be expressed in an exaggerated form.

Most of life practically depends on balance of functions and self-knowledge, along with this is urgently needed a sense of relative proportion in our activities emphasis, and the *gradual* development of a sense of synthesis of our structure-function-order, and how it can gear in *consciously* with the larger structure-function-order of the universe we call "God."

This, practically speaking, means developing the skill and ability of fitting forces to functions through coherent forms - be they of thinking, feeling, doing, etc. Control and direction and intelligent understanding of the processes, practices, and persistence necessary to acquire this should be made a large part of any functional education with most of the emphasis on *function*, not ideas, verbalisms, concepts, opinions, traditions and empty words.

A functional understanding and gradual growth-through-application of the law of three is a very useful and necessary tool that has to be built, developed and applied to most daily situations; the factors of balance, the feel for synthesis and right proportional function must be bred in the bone, absorbed into the blood, and eventually expressed easily in most of our speech, thought, feeling and actions.

Given intelligent effort, proper use of time-space and understanding of the cyclic nature of the events in our lives; given the gradual growth and strengthening of our basic consciousness - then the path to integrated living can be entered upon with some reasonable expectation of stable growth, increasing awareness, more effective functioning, better relationships with others, and the development of enough perceptive insight and power to build the kind of life congruent to our basic needs, structures and abilities - and not depolarized by the chaos all around.

Ideas which are not connected to any structure; which are vast blind verbalizations having nothing to do with our present structure and needs; ideas which enthuse us, blind us, wipe out our discriminative and selective faculties; which trigger us off to unmeasured, unstructured and un-rhythmic action - these are amongst the greatest menaces to survival that we all face today.

Our natural state is that of Cosmos - a beauty and an order. When we allow ourselves to live otherwise, we invite varying degrees of trouble.

We can become so hypnotized by an idea or ideas that we become electrically ungrounded - we lose our contact with the actual Here-Now of the structural universe in which we live. This then must lead either to no function or malfunction in daily life - both equally undesirable.

Symbols may or may not be ornamental, but their fundamental purpose is for practical use by intelligent energies.

A true symbol is:

- a body containing a soul
- matter holding a meaning
- a focus of force
- a condenser of consciousness
- a "thought-tank" - anything and everything can be a symbol.

Magical symbols are fundamental concepts for energy exchanges between very different levels (or "worlds") of living, and the intelligent beings operating through them.

In ancient Egypt, the symbols of geometry denoted *functions*. True symbolism, if it is to follow the natural order and be a true guide for growth, should deal primarily with functions. Where ideas rather than functions become paramount, action, growth and applied understanding become vitiated.

It is the energy, meaning, associations and life-force you pack into any symbol that makes it alive and functional for you. By itself it is nothing.

The gradual outgrowing of the low emotional levels; the removing of your energy from identification with your emotions; the plugging up of most unconscious emotional leaks - these are the essence of growth and infinitely more important to proper function than any idea's glittering promise.

The attaining of a stable conscious focus in all you do; the constant nourishing of your deeper inner being with the higher-level frequencies from the Noetic level; the setting up of a stable, pulsing, alternating and cosmically true and healthful rhythm in your daily life - these will carry you far on the road to the gods of order and light, co-worker with the eternal forces.

A conscious awareness of what you are doing, and when and where you are doing it; a steadfast, conscious refusal to leak or waste thought or feeling energy on anything automatic and useless; a gradual reining in and diminishing of your automatic, compulsive, impulsive and unconscious speech - these three should be constant daily companions in your travel on the process road to the place of light (Noetic levels).

The root purpose of becoming more conscious and aware in *everything* you *do* and *say* should be fixed in your mind, engraved on your heart and powerfully applied by your hands - this is a true divine marriage.

Today most of our educational institutions, religious teachings, business and family ideals have become empty, meaningless and hollow shells incapable of furnishing true soul nourishment in any degree. So, for the true learner there is no alternative - either seek or die.

De-hypnosis, de-conditioning and finally detachment from words as *having any inherent meaning in themselves* - this is a tremendous and vital step towards living and functioning in perception; as a seer (see-er, true clair-voyant or clear see-er).

Words, concepts, thoughts, opinions, ideas - these, in identification are the components of man's immersion in the maya (delusion, false values and evaluations based on identifications with images in the mind made substantive.)

Identification with unconscious second order abstractions (words) not only cause a legion of "diseases," but makes sane function practically impossible. By sane function we mean function in accordance with the natural order - an energy being living and doing in a vast dynamic energy process-complex called the "world."

Perception (sanity) and ideas (delusions) are in inverse ratio - these calls for a disciplined training in the consciousness of abstracting.

Words and the unconscious associations which they trigger off:

- pull you out of present time awareness, which is not good.
- waste much energy uselessly.
- create delusions and false-to-fact evaluations in you.
- dim and often short-circuit your awareness.
- prevent clear perception of the coordinates of the present environment.
- cause malfunction in your sensory-motor nervous system, thus causing improper response to the present event in which you are participating.

Most of the above negatives can be overcome through study of Korzybski's general semantics and training in functioning as an energy being living in a dynamic energy world.

You cannot drink the word water; you cannot eat the word steak; yet, because of our not understanding the mechanism of abstracting on different levels, words can shove us around like puppets - set up uncontrolled reactions in us that can be very damaging to our health.

Words and concepts seem to have become substitutes for living experiences - words are being used, speech being amplified at a tremendous rate because of the electronic news media. The movies and newspapers and magazines all add their quota to our organized ignorance, more threatening to our sane existence than any atom bomb could be.

Intentional orientation (looking for "meaning" in words and juggling verbal noises in a mad, blind hope to make sense out of events and things) actually creates and perpetuates ignorance and delusion by its very nature and *frustrates* us.

Extensional orientation (looking for and working with life-facts - structure-function-order of Cosmos) gradually brings more sanity and creative energy back into our lives. If, in our daily use of words, we omit making a stable context; if we do not bother to validate the meanings of the verbal sounds we use, then our unconsciousness of proper word use creates a Frankenstein which can destroy us at a gradually accelerating rate.

When engaged in any activity around unconscious people; when in any large gathering whether of the family, theater, sports, etc.; when shopping in the supermarkets, STAY IN THE PERCEPTIVE COGNITION STATE (not thinking, reviewing the past, images, etc.). It seems to be some kind of a natural law that unconscious people set up and generate all kinds of negative events from minor accidents to national-international chaos, war and destruction.

It seems to be a truism that an unconscious person's offer of help turns into a factual thrust to destroy and demolish. Advice from unconscious people (especially reformers, teachers, etc.) is most often unbalanced, fragmented, deluded, personal, ignorant and bestial and can only reflect the inner (and outer) chaos in which they themselves "live." It is extremely dangerous to listen to this when you are tired and in a low energy state.

You should train to make your mind completely attentive to the Here-Now in everyday living. After a while, this grows into a natural state and you have built a partial protection from getting sucked into the vortices of negative function-events created by these unconscious people. (The Bible calls them the living dead; and makes the statement: "Let the dead bury the dead; life is for the living.") Those who wander from the path of understanding (self-knowledge and awareness) shall never leave the congregation of the dead.

Opinions that are so strong in you that you express unconsciously must be gradually brought under *conscious* control; your base of operations should slowly but persistently be raised from automatic thought-feeling concepts to direct perception of what is. Try to plug up *all* wasteful leaks in you - physically, emotionally, mentally, spiritually.

For all practical purposes, God is synonymous with the principle of balance. To this we add a sense of synthesis, plus a strong feel for general semantics.

Given these three, the beginnings of a sane and ordered life become possible.

However, the way is difficult, tedious and long - persistence, intense preparation and endless effort will carry you far on the way; but of course, much more is needed.

Potentially, the way is for everyone. In actual practice, this way is only for the few - those who are awakening feel the need for integration in their bones and are willing to sweat out the restructuring process necessary before the Christos (higher frequencies) can enter properly.

When any person is neither ripe nor ready, all talk about the higher life is not only foolish and wasted, but dangerous.

Unconscious projection of our thoughts, feelings, ideas, concepts, etc., is *exceedingly* prevalent and strong in the early growth stages of the struggle towards the light. We must develop enough inner strength and awareness to gradually diminish this automatic projection.

Much strength, both inner and outer, must be developed and is vitally needed to be able to sustain the shock of our delusions - strength not to be repelled at the vast ugliness, bestiality and unconsciousness that becomes more apparent as we progress, and also strength not to be deluded and attracted by the growing, though transient, beauty that we see all around.

It is essential not to be thrown off our center by anything we see or contact in the outer world, and also in the inner world of subjective ideas and feelings. A point of balance which can oscillate as needed but then return to its center should be developed.

The attention must perennially be worked, trained and super-honed to notice more and more details at any focus point at which it is chosen to function; a clean, flexible, strong and *aware* control must be developed; reasoning by coordinated and proportionate thinking should be practiced until they become second nature.

It is *of the essence* to gradually wean yourself away from a *priori thinking and reasoning*.

A *priori* thinking means basing your statements on hypotheses and theories, rather than on experiment and experiences.

Since a *priori* thinking and reasoning so often is against the natural order; since it increases gullibility, self-deception, lying and laziness; and, most important, it precludes validation in life-facts and living experiences, it is the height of wisdom to gradually phase it out of your life completely.

When you leave or are pulled from your basic center, there remains little or no protection in your aura from the chaotic force fields and destructive emotions so prevalent in our unbalanced society.

Regain your center - take a few soft, deep, rhythmic breaths, go into perception of where you are rather than thinking. This will detune you from the negative around you and help you consciously tune into the higher levels of the frequencies.

We would caution you that every magical experiment flies from the public, seeking to be hid; it is strengthened and confirmed by silence, but is destroyed by publication.

Unconscious rapports on the physical, emotional and mental levels motivate, push into action, direct and control practically the entire lives of over 99% of the people - as long as one has *not* individualized, or is in process therein, he is completely at the mercy of the motion picture (first order abstractions) going on in his head.

In today's world, to permit yourself to lose, or stray from, your physical, mental, emotional calm-poise regularly is to place your whole life and future in grave danger.

Perhaps one of the greatest menaces we face today is the identification with, and use of, ideas-concepts-words *without* a stable context based on the natural order; the proliferation of word-noises and attempts to explain anything deep through words only must inevitably set forces into motion which will tend to bring about an ever-accelerating chaos, fear, antagonism, then destruction. Agitated news, TV programs, magazines, books, social media, etc., all combine to form a poisoned curtain of ignorance which becomes ever more disturbed and fragmented by mouth noises posing as words. Without some kind of referent set up consciously, practically all that comes out of the collective mouth is nothing more than raw unconscious noise creating delusion and verbal sewage that pollute the inner thought streams and infect action.

Automatic and unconscious word-forms that flit through your mind from who knows where, agitate your mind and feelings and trigger you into unconscious action; cause you to engage in non-functional and non-relevant actions, wasting your energy, weakening and damaging your sense of choice, depolarizing you from your life-goal of becoming an integrated individual - scattering and unfocusing your will, thought and wisdom forces to such a degree that you begin to resonate with, and be governed by, the forces of chaos and disharmony so prevalent in today's world.

A master-sense of integrated function should be slowly and carefully built up in you. This becomes a kind of radar map-guide that keeps you focused, directed and constantly aware of your true, deeper inner goal. This can eventually act as a compass by means of which you navigate around or through the stormy waters of fragmented living into the safe harbor of relevant, integrated daily function.

Man is as stupid about himself as he is intelligent about his machines and technologies.

Obsessed and possessed by his *own* unconscious thought-forms and feeling-forms, the average person walks around in an acrid and blinding smog (self-created) which effectively screens out and prevents most sane, reasoned and decent behavior because of one's identifications and so, misevaluations, of the thoughts he thinks, the emotions he feels, and the unconscious reactions to outside stimuli which make of him a total puppet automatically dancing and speaking almost totally controlled by outer sensations, speech and hypnotic suggestions.

Well over 98% of most people's thoughts, feelings, ideas, concepts, opinions and words are, from a *work* standpoint, ignorant, useless, wasted, chaotic and fomenters and creators of chaos, confusion and eventual destruction.

Hard, persistent and intelligent study, work, and recollection will eventually release a person from domination (unconscious) by words, concepts, thoughts, etc.- the prison of the personality and identification with ideas in the mind made substantive.

Repeat to yourself dozens of times daily, if necessary: "words have *no* inherent or intrinsic meaning of *any* kind. For decent and natural order communication, it is urgent that the speaker on *any* useful topic set up conscious referents for every important link and word in his speech."

Burn into your consciousness: language and word-usage must be modeled after, and conform to, the natural order - that is, the *way* the universe functions. Work mostly and continually with life-facts and you will find the hazy fog of ideas and word-noises lifting from your awareness, leaving you capable of and free to perceive and know.

Ignorant and bestial parents; unconscious animals whose higher centers are sealed; *completely* governed by the lower centers of appetite, sensation, sex and greed, create ignorant and bestial little children - destructive, unconscious, animal-reactive types who grow up into ignorant, destructive and bestial adults, totally controlled and run by their uncontrolled passions and ignorant identifications with symbols in the mind made substantive.

It is sometimes possible, at the cost of great pain and suffering, for these children to change as they grow older; however, so great is the power of the old subconscious habits, so vast is the subconscious ignorance of proper natural order function, that perhaps 1/100 of 1% make it - the rest become, more or less, unconscious destructive models molded totally by daily contact.

The life-focus and basic point of consciousness determine automatically what a person is, does, thinks, feels and acts.

It is extremely dangerous in this culture to be unaware of the beast-forces, ignorance, bestiality, brutality and obsession which is the NORM for this society and this "culture."

Practically *every* institution based on the Piscean Age ideas and coordinates is functionally inadequate to handle today's needs and requirements. Also, the imposing by *force* of these brutal and improper rules, laws and concepts makes a very bad situation many times worse.

It is *structurally impossible* to expect anything rational, adequate, decent and sane from most of our institutions on *every level*.

Our everyday archaic, false-to-fact deceptive and completely inadequate Aristotelian language patterns are rather rapidly destroying the benefits of a science approach.

We don't yet see clearly how an archaic, elemental, false-to-fact and non-functional Aristotelian language structure puts sand in the gears of all our everyday relationships; how we continually and dangerously identify with every word-noise, thus *automatically* making false evaluations. These evaluations continually create accidents in daily life in the same way that mis-evaluating the distance between our car and the cars on both sides of us on the freeway will cause an accident.

The reality of any "thing" is its structure-function-order; all the opinions, thoughts, words, ideas, concepts and verbalisms about it not congruent to this structure-function-order triad is just so much sand in the gears of a motor - malfunction and final breakdown must be the ultimate result. Not only does this happen continually daily but we identify with word-noises having no substance in reality and bitterly bewail when things go wrong.

The Hermetic path, through the development, stabilization and use of the trained mind is really the most basic and proper for these days.

For, though a man may make living contact with the elemental powers behind nature, and another may achieve a mystical contact with deep spiritual reality, yet, unless the mind has been trained, all the results of such contacts will inevitably be distorted and misapplied on the physical plane.

The true mysteries are experienced, not taught, and cannot be communicated to others by words.

The delusion, illusion and confusion created and maintained by identification with words-thoughts-concepts-ideas is absolutely incredible and cannot be verbally represented. But the negative, destructive, chaotic and insane conditions thus created is completely shocking once realized in its proper proportion.

All written and spoken language is an abstraction of an abstraction; when we abstract consciously, we grow in communicative skill and understanding.

Unconscious abstractions automatically open a Pandora's box of imps from hell who immediately set forth gleefully on a destructive holiday.

The energy wasted and misdirected in negative emotions and emotional thinking could, if used properly, move the world a giant step to sanity and intelligent cooperation.

Look how powerfully the written and spoken word affect us - reactions, usually blind, unconscious and unstructured, out of *ALL* proportion to the congruence of the word to the actual point-event, are triggered off automatically and push us into the verbal, then action, stereotypes that are very wrong for our true function and future.

Words as of the present stage of man's development are tools necessary to certain functions. However, if their use and structure and mechanics are not properly understood - if our attention *is not trained* to become stronger than the word-symbol - we then function invertedly - run more by word-noises than by operational structures and energies.

Words can blind us, heat us, cool us, make us act and react like zombies or puppets - make us *totally waste* our God-given and precious energy unconsciously and automatically. They thus steal from us the substance-force necessary to transmute our beings to higher levels (the Christos and beyond).

Mostly, words heard, written and used unconsciously, because they generate mis-evaluations and false-to-fact thoughts-actions in us are perhaps our greatest prison.

It sometimes seems that mis-used and out of context words create more disease, sickness, ill-health and destruction than all the combined germs in the world.

It is *vitally imperative* that any seeker after true life-wisdom see clearly how utterly deluded, trapped, harassed and made frustrated people become through wrong use of words, thoughts, ideas and concepts.

Practice by small, easy, conscious degrees, non-reactivity to words and the automatic impulses they conjure up in us. Realize, in your very bones, that approximately well over 90% of the words in general usage (on TV, in business, the home, etc., etc., etc.) have no actual referent in reality. They are shadows of shadows of shadows without any substance in reality.

Thinking, feeling and reacting to words unconsciously; *a priori* thinking applied to present environmental needs guarantee that frustration, malfunction, chaos and eventually death must eventuate.

Much time and effort should be spent on gradually realizing the insidious danger and grave peril inherent in *a priori* reasoning (reasoning by hypotheses and theories, without checking for life-facts and natural order functioning).

A priori thinking creates a delusion breeding, opaque wall between the person and the reality of whatever he/she is talking about - in general semantics this is called intentional orientation (focused on words and ideas) rather than on life-facts and empirical data gained by observation, testing, experimenting and *continually* checking the words-ideas-concepts against the living universe of patterned and interpenetrating energies and structures.

Facts come before theories; *a priori* thinking creates theories and hypotheses endlessly; then amplifies them endlessly; then creates a nebulous fog in which the theory maker gets lost.

We are here to earn and birth a consciousness; an individuality polarized to and functioning in the Noetic level (true light, true mind) of being.

The first business of consciousness is *perception*, to acquire which is both a tremendous amount of work, and skill of ultimate importance to your deeper growth into the light.

The next step is *recording*; this again is a tremendous skill acquired by intense training, practice and application to all the necessary daily functions - on whatever levels necessary.

After that, we can go to *thinking* and automatically we enter the field of geometry - the use of symbols correlated to *functions*, not rootless ideas which not being correlated to the natural order create endless confusion and misery.

A true symbol (according to the deeper Egyptian tradition) is a geometry of functions; ideas not congruent to the structure of the natural order cause physical-mental short circuits in a person's head like wrong connections in any electrical machine would cause it to malfunction - to either stop or slow up, function improperly and probably cause damage to the user and anyone else in the immediate neighborhood.

We have, practically speaking, very little choice. Either we model and structure our thinking after the life facts of the Cosmic Order and are sustained and strengthened, or we think any ideas automatically absorbed from a usually negative and destructive environment. This automatically puts wrong voltages, currents and resistances inside the electrical circuitry of the body. This in turn causes almost an infinity of diseases, misfortunes and chaos.

Symbols that are not structured properly; not connected, measured and ordered according to life-facts; *not* related *consciously* to function - these are actually and potentially a very great danger and threat to anyone who really wants to lead an integrated and balanced life. A true symbol, properly related to the natural order, can bring in much new and healing life-force. A symbol unconsciously made and unconsciously used most often places so much death (unconsciousness) into its user.

Unconscious symbols, like thieves in the night, rob you of so much life-force, time, energy, capacity and ability to order your living towards the true Gnosis.

These improperly made and unconsciously used symbols:

- deteriorate, weaken and destroy the nervous system.
- cause unending chaos in the everyday life through a malfunctioning nervous system which is supposed to correlate the outer events to the person's inner registry and reality.

It is urgently important in these days of total and massive hypnosis, conditioning and manipulation of purely verbal symbols that one shift his functioning by degrees away from a focus in intentional orientation (idea and word focus) to extensional orientation (focus on the actual events, facts and space-time continuum in which the point-events occur).

As you learn to diminish the vast delusion and waste of your *a priori* thinking, a whole new world of perception and function begins to open. As you move towards extensional orientation in your daily life, your energy can increase greatly - your conscious awareness released from the bondage and prison of fixed concepts, words, ideas and dogma-opinions, begins to expand, clarify, awaken, sharpen and become more original. Truly you begin to be reborn, perception-wise.

Snap judgments made on the spur of the moment, allowing no time for the impressions, facts and frequencies to enter into us more completely, not only create more delusion, but store up negative karma that will have to be paid for, sooner or later.

Identification with words and verbal forms not only puts thick sand in the machinery of everyday function, it tunes you to a seething vortex of negative expressions and feelings which corrodes you on the inner levels and destroys clear perception on the outer planes.

In anything important in your life, it should be made an iron-clad rule to set up precise and structured referents for the words you are using to communicate with others. Otherwise, mistakes, hostility, wrong understanding, and so wrong function, become inevitable.

The heartache, suffering, chaos, destruction and pure insane murder caused by identification with words-thoughts-images-ideas-concepts (*all* maya, *all pure* delusion) *cannot* be chronicled verbally or by any written form. Only seeing the effects daily in the destruction of people's deepest needs, hopes and goals can give a tiny glimpse of the terrible havoc wreaked by unconscious abstracting, *a priori* thinking and intentional orientation.

We are here to work co-measuredly, to grow in understanding of God (the natural order of cosmos), to make knowing contact with the higher forces and become conscious co-creators with them.

Then, after due preparation, we may earn the privilege of grounding and making available some of the purposes and plans of the Shining Ones on the physical planes.

It is wise not to place *too* much attention on the anguish torn, debilitating, chaotic, unsane, delusion-breeding and negative-emotional vortices that we see all around us in the mass media, literature and especially that snake-pit of visual masturbation called TV. Perhaps later more constructive things may come from it - but, functionally, as of now, it is perhaps one of the major sources of people pollution and degradation in the country. The poisonous suggestion and powerful impact of the sex-crime-violence programs continually bombarding the mass-mind daily; the vicious vomit of emotionally hypnotized, negatively polarized TV announcements on the news programs; the constant stimulating of fear, worry, hate, doubt and anxiety that is created by these programs and then fed to the helpless and hypnotized viewer - this is a people pollutant greater and more destructive than anything in recorded history.

God is slowness; the devil (for these times) is speed and the concomitant ignorance and chaos that it thus generates. Since time is the interval between seed and fruit (in everything and all our activities), we then literally create and ignite our own destruction through wrong evaluation of the co-ordinates of all our relationships. From this it is but a short step to complete unconsciousness in all our daily functions, relationships and actions. This is also another name for complete insanity and must bring dire consequences as automatically as a lit match dropped on a pile of dry hay immediately causes a roaring conflagration almost impossible to control.

The development of patience, poise, peace, persistence at the center of our being is not only a true path to clear perceptions, it is also the only real path to sanity in our daily life.

As one's sensitivity to the higher magnetic fields increases, one sees and senses much more in the everyday environment. As the distorting veils of identifications with your thoughts, feelings, actions, words, ideas and concepts gradually wear away, perception of the real (basic energy patterns and structures) slowly increases. As one finds this happening, many things that once could be done must be stopped - you have become a more sensitized receiver, hence the coordinates of your working functions have changed.

New senses are tapped into, gradually trained and finally applied more or less skillfully in everyday living.

The change-over, better done slowly, from the agitation and heat of delusory emotion driven thinking (heated and unconscious mainly) to the clarity and coolness of perceptive cognition is a major breakthrough from unconscious slavery to the beginning of conscious function.

Any and all meditation on words only in search of meaning generates terrific chaos and confusion in a person's mind.

Instead let us *examine-feel-sense-perceive* the structure-function-order of what is around us and so realize that we are dynamic units of energy in a tremendous energy process.

All words are abstractions and have no inherent meanings. When we give a deep, compulsive or "inherent" meaning to any word we are then reifying. This then becomes a mis-evaluation (false-to-facts data) upon which we base our thinking and acting. Since our thinking-acting is based upon a delusion and unreality, we set into motion a negative set of circumstances which in turn clobber us destructively.

We must structure our language to coincide with the natural order (this is a conscious process) and establish referents for all the important words.

Ideas, ideals, concepts and symbols that are not congruent to and correlated with the cosmos and its natural order are exceedingly dangerous, damaging and harmful. Since everything in the natural order is related in a certain measure and proportion, we have dependable function, order and structure on which to stabilize our lives and grow and share the evolving light within us. However, ideas-ideals that are not correlated with and coordinated to the natural order are like a drunken driver who weaves in and out of both the north bound and south bound lanes, at his own sweet will, in total disregard of traffic conditions all around him. Inevitably he must cause accidents. The saddest part of which is the fact that, besides destroying himself, he can harm and kill many innocent people. A true symbol in Cosmos delineates function - anything less or other merely breeds delusion, chaos, ignorance, fear, eventual misevaluation and finally destruction.

Society today is becoming increasingly vulnerable to and increasingly harmed by the use of swindlers algebra. That is, symbols are used to motivate action and move people which do not have any referent in reality. They do, however, inflame the desires and cause unmeasured, automatic and un-sane action which then of course, breeds malfunction, misery and mass insanity.

It is urgently important to orientate yourself to an energy-world functioning in all that you say, hear, feel and do. As long as the main focus of your consciousness is on words-ideas-opinions, you will continue to be glued to the delusion (the maya) of words and appearances of the outer world as real. Heartache, heartbreak and fear will dog your footsteps.

Until one acquires the practical skill of functional synthesis in everyday life, the Gnosis must remain a sealed book to you - synthesis, function, energies are big keys.

CLEAR THINKING

STAR LAUNCH 16

Watch your breath, so your mind can be
From emotion's turmoil constantly free Jangling thoughts
and uneven breath Increase delusions and lead to death.

Power your mind with poise and calm
So your days and ways can lead to the balm
Of rhythmic function and balanced order
That carries you high to True Heaven's border.

Look not to ideas, or concept, or word
Lest you fall in the maelstrom of the boiling herd
Of measure and reason completely void
By their negative forces totally destroyed.

Your prison is your thought and feeling
that blinds perception, sets judgement reeling
Into the morass of confusion-doubt
So that idea insanities you only spout.

Automatic word, and action and thought
In mindless unreason forever caught
Parrots screaming Einstein's theory
Till Wisdom dies and the soul grows weary.

Isidore Friedman

THERE ARE CERTAIN BASIC RULES FOR GOOD thinking which, although simple, are very important.

These rules are:

- Do no try to plan, structure or formulate a new development late at night. Don't try to *solve* anything. Remember timing and ripeness are most everything in a new, or any, project.

- Never try to solve any deep problem when you are tired, upset, angry, depressed, excited, enthusiastic, unconscious, worried, fearful, doubtful, etc., etc. Try to wait till your energy is high and you are in a good inner-outer state before thinking through a new procedure.

- *Never* ask advice or take advice, or consult with an excited, emotionally polarized or unconsciously enthusiastic person. They are off balance and unconscious.

- Especially avoid consulting or asking advice from people who are easily excitable and regularly indulge in extravagant speech. People that rapidly switch moods and argue all the time should be calmly avoided.

- People who constantly quote "authorities" or "experts" in the field to prove their prejudices should be avoided.

- Infantile people who are run by their emotions also must be handled with care; also people who immediately spew out an opinion or judgment without any time for examining the question or finding out the basic coordinates and facts of the problem under discussion.

- People that are careless with small details; that promise quickly and then forget, or do not do what they say or promise - again much care is advised in dealing with them, especially trusting them.

- People who make extravagant promises one day, and conveniently forget the next day; people who always rush to start something into motion without careful observation and thought, these most often cause many severe problems in human relations, and very often cannot be trusted or depended upon to follow through on what they said.

- People with a weak attention, hasty observation - who reason by words, emotions and ideas rather than observed and tested facts - they are automatic trouble-makers.

- Especially must you be cautious with anyone who makes statements on hearsay, who triggers off and gets upset, angry or pleased at the slightest trifle - these are hooked into chaos and confusion, and will spread it to you and allow them ingress into your mind and feelings.

- You should be extra careful with *any* written contract, guarantee or important papers to *thoroughly check* each word for specific references - take nothing for granted.

- Be sure the language is crystal clear in your mind - otherwise something inferred or imagined that was taken for granted by you can boomerang back and cause much loss, grief, inconvenience, and financial difficulties.

- In any important plan, project or construction, check, double-check and recheck constantly as the process of working out the details of the plan goes on. This can save you much grief, money, lost time and wasted energy.

- Never allow yourself to be rushed or brainwashed into a hurried action or decision. Take time to think through the various "X" aspects that must always show up on more attentive, slower, and more careful examination. Well over 85% of our problems would either never happen, or vanish completely, if we just slowed down, applied bare attention, detailed and good observation, and good (measured and unemotional) reasoning to all our goals, circumstances, relations and activities.

NATURAL ORDER NOTES

STAR FRUIT 13

Balance is your guiding star
The Christos sent from aeons afar
To show the way of the teacher, pain
That you may integrate in the cosmic chain.

Matter is blended form and force
A collector of Light from Original Source
Spirit and matter are string and sound
Through balance, their cosmic harmony abound.

The positive, the negative, then the blend
With skillful action the chaos mend
The opposites joined, no more oppose
The being can rest in balanced repose.

And create, through Light, some part of the plan
In the conscious growth of the more-than-man
Who then becomes antenna for
The godling's new wings, infra-dimensional soar.

To the Timeless-Structure that calls to man
To do his part in the aeonic plan
To co-create, with the powers-that-be
The next proper chapter in Eternity.

Isidore Friedman

THERE IS NO NEED TO CLIMB GIANT MOUNTAINS, fly to the moon, rocket to other planets - all that we need to learn and grow into our true heritage as Conscious Beings (Christos) is all around us in our everyday circumstances, relations and work.

The Higher Forces have placed all the secrets, miracles and wonders of the universe in the one place that guarantees our never seeing or finding them - right in front of our eyes and noses. There they stand, *completely* hidden because they are so obvious we can't see them.

The deeper secrets are also hidden in these familiar objects: the rainbow, the magnet, the corkscrew, the top, the human body, the snail, breathing, the volute, water, fire, earth, air, snow and rain, letters and numbers.

Nature has been called the First Science - God the first Scientist. By keeping our eyes and ears *open* and our mouths shut; by staying in bare attention and really looking at things; by non-reacting; by slowing down – Nature's book opens and clearly teaches us *untold* miracles.

Notice the alternation between day and night; between in-breath and out-breath; between work and rest; between storm and clear skies; between strain and relaxation; between joy and sorrow; between peace and abrasive daily toil; between hunger and satiety. In the wave lies hid the secret of the universe.

The beautiful symbol of the I Ching: the yang and the yin; the hard and the soft; the creative and the receptive; the birth and the death. Each pole contains the seed of its opposite; and changes to its opposite.

YANG
HEAVEN

YIN
EARTH

Everything changes; the entire world Process is composed of change which is "thinging" (making things); nothing stands still; everything pulsates and alternates; all is flux and flow; to and fro; fixation becomes death. We should train ourselves to breathe things in, then breathe them out.

We can only reach illumination through learning and handling *properly* our every-day circumstances. As the Chinese say, "The Tao (way) is our every day." Life is not thought, or speech or pretty words and concepts; it is a sturdy treading of the everyday in peace, strength, wisdom, light and overcoming of our beast ignorance and animal nature.

There is no mystery to anything, *if* we keep our eyes open, stay in bare attention constantly, become non-reactive; make our attention *stronger* than any symbol, idea, word, event, or P.P.P. (Pressure Points of the Past) - and practice "obnosis" (the observation of the obvious) regularly and intelligently.

Our purpose in life is to become, gradually, prepared to enter the fifth kingdom, the kingdom of Souls - of Light. Just as there is a *vast* difference between plant and animal; and even vaster difference between animal and man, so is there a vast difference between a man and a Soul - Sun of God.

After having learned true Magic - which is ever *the price that has been paid* - one becomes a Soul - a conscious co-creator with the Higher Forces, a sharer of the purpose, energy and meaning of our Creator in ever higher, wider and more expansive octaves of being and becoming.

We work, slowly and painfully, from being sons of darkness (S.O.D.) to becoming and *earning* the privileges of sons of Light (S.O.L.) We must *first* become octave-beings, tuned to the Cosmic Scale, before we can make beautiful music on our body-mind instrument; and serve *properly*.

We are *always* dealing with the observer's consciousness and his knowledge of his perceptual mechanisms. In other words, his level of awareness and his instruments of perception. Now, a person's level of consciousness will *always* affect how, what, where and when and who he sees on *all* levels.

Always remember: Reality is non-verbal; living is non-verbal; experience is non-verbal; facts are non-verbal; true life-relations are non-verbal. You receive *much more* on the non-verbal *silent frequency* level of any situation than from all the words in the dictionary.

Try to *constantly* bear in mind the constant, root importance of becoming and staying *conscious*, in ever-widening arcs of awareness. Most people live, love, write, work, talk, think, feel and act in a complete state of unconsciousness. Consciousness is a vital, alert, strong state of *wordless* awareness.

ORGANICS
FOR
EVERYDAY LIVING

STAR SEED BETA 11

Rouse the rainbow in your heart
That a cosmic life may truly start
Wake the sleeping god within
To crack the mind-idols of brittle tin.

Know – Will – Dare - and Do
Such is the path for the very few
Let the infinite hunger in you rise
To taste the soul food in the skies.

But first the cup must be thoroughly clean
Purged from its dross, a mind serene
A balanced living bred in the bone
Perceptive cognition of the Inner Tone.

A calm but steady study make,
Of the spiral forces that universes wake.
Take silence into your very marrow
That the Lighted Pattern may guide your thought-arrow.

Penetrate, like a laser beam,
Into the center of your dream
Then tune and tone your questing ray
To touch and travel the God's Structured Way.

Isidore Friedman

EVERYTHING IN YOUR LIFE DEPENDS ON HOW YOU handle the co-ordinates in your day by day living.

A good practice to get into is to break your life into 24-hour compartments, or sections. Then learn to handle each section and its particular problems, events, needs and situations right then and there, consciously. Live in the "what is," not in the "what was," (the past) or the "what will be" (the future). The past is gone, learn from it and forget it. The future is not here yet, plan it intelligently and don't worry about it.

In short, it is a question of pure physics (and geometry), applied to everyday things.

Practice giving each situation and event its exact amount of time and energy, no more, no less (physics - work in = work out, no waste). Learn to use the Law of the Triangle (law of three) in all your daily activities - i.e., 1. you; 2. the thing, event, person, problem, etc.; 3. the relationship between.

You have a limited, set, finite amount of energy. You (and no one else) have to arrange the space-time, matter-energy co-ordinates to reach your goals.

Picture yourself like an electrical battery with "X" amount of energy available. Once you realize this, the next step is to learn to co-ordinate your daily life so that each goal is given the right amount of energy according to its PRIORITY in your life. Energize the important things in your life first.

All the concepts, words, ideas, hopes, sayings, verbalism, faith, (all verbal and spoken knowledge) is utterly *useless* and inadequate if not tied into an intelligent, ordered, structured and functional *doing* and *handling* of your energies and the day's events and conditions.

The real Truth is "Faith without action is dead." You can idealize, hope, think, talk, etc. all you want that your problems and situations will work themselves out, BUT unless you add that magic ingredient "action" or more accurately "coordinated action" it is all useless.

All ideas are equated with *insanity*, if they are not tied into a proper matrix and structure to include functional *doing* - faith by itself is not only stupid, inadequate, useless, helpless and wrong - it is absolutely *dangerous* if not tied in with intelligent work and energy.

We live in a functional ordered universe of forces, forms and structures and relationships, NOT a universe of ideas. In reality, man-made ideas have no natural order structure or function. Anyone pursuing such an ungrounded idea is dangerous - the blind continuous pursuit of it can only lead to chaos and insanity.

Faith, by itself alone, if not co-ordinated with conscious effort, work on oneself, intelligent planning, measurement of the structure-function-order of your daily life and needs, is not only complete madness, but a not so subtle form of spiritual parasitism when the person sits with his hands under his fanny and expects "God" to do all for him.

To rely on faith alone is to misunderstand the natural-order-functioning of God's plan and His universe. Faith must in its natural-order lead to confidence, confidence in your ability to *do*. But to do correctly, in the natural-order of that particular event.

All ideas that are not tied to a structure and co-ordinated into a clean, practical space-time, energy-matter matrix are also insane and will always make you lose your energy uselessly, waste your time, become unfocused to practical everyday needs, besides opening you up to every delusion under the sun, negating and nullifying your every plan, goal and hope - and making frustration your constant companion.

Every event or situation has, generally speaking, correct structure and co-ordinates to be followed for its practical and successful completion. These correct solutions usually take the least amount of time and energy. To not follow these proper structures is to use and waste energy and thereby in the long run frustrate and confuse you.

Hopes, desires, needs, goals, necessities, that are not backed up by constant, conscious, intelligent and persistent doing and working, can never be fulfilled. Energy output can only be equal to energy input minus the losses due to resistance and poor co-ordination. If you don't plant the seeds of intelligent effort and co-ordinated synthesis in the S-T-E-M (Space-Time-Energy-Matter) world, you can never reap the fruits of your goals.

Remember you can't get "something for nuthin." To achieve your hopes, desires, goals and needs "pay the proper price." Don't ask for or seek shortcuts. Pay the price of intelligent effort and co-ordinated action and reap your own rewards.

You must become a miser and hoard your energy totally - it is your controlled and stored and directed energy, used properly in correct *sequence* and phase that will bring you to your true needs and heart's goal. It is *not* love, ideas, hope, faith and all that other verbal baloney, which in reality are only noises - reifications (saying words until you begin to think they are things) - then delusion sets in.

In reality you are a dynamic unit of energy in a dynamic field. You have a finite amount of energy - learn how to use it wisely. Plug up all the frivolous leaks of your precious energy. Your energy is your Prime Mover and without your energy all your love, ideas, hope, faith are useless (dead words).

The more you look at and wonder about, and get ideas about - what other guys are doing and saying -

and start thinking, "Well maybe they have the *secret*" - (well there is no secret - and no magic - there is only *the price that has been paid*) the more lost and helpless you will get.

The secret of the universe (if you are still looking for a secret), is that you will get whatever you need if you are willing to pay the price, in conscious, correct and natural order effort. It is smarter to work for what you need, rather than fill your life with what you think you want because the prices to be paid are not always visible ones. Every living being on this planet has his own individual destiny and path, it is insane and unnatural to try to follow someone else's.

Your accomplishments will be in inverse ratio to the amount of talk - the more talk, the *less* the accomplishment, when you talk a lot you:

- waste energy stupidly
- confuse yourself or the other person
- delude yourself or the other
- lie to yourself or the other
- substitute talk for action and get no where.

Physical work is not the only way to use up energy; talking uses energy, actually spurious talking wastes energy. An ancient truth to be practiced by all is "silence is golden." Use your energy intelligently in "right action."

Be extra careful that you do *not set more things* into motion than your structure can handle properly.

Try to set up a very smooth cycle of start-maintain-end in all your activities. Do *not* keep starting things automatically, thinking maybe, maybe. Maybe right now is for *consolidation*. Not expanding.

Do not "bite off more than you can chew." If a project is worth starting it is worth finishing. Do less things than usual, but do them well. Remember whatever you sow (start), you must reap (consciously or unconsciously).

Do not *delude* yourself about making one big killing and getting out from under the mountain of debts which your unconsciousness and greed have accumulated - steady, conscious and consolidated work will set you out of it.

Whatever position you find yourself in today, remember you caused it, no one else. It may have taken years or even lifetimes to put you where you are now. If you don't like where you are, you must change your ways, and slowly, steadily, consciously work your way out. Remember "inch by inch life's a cinch; yard by yard, life's too hard."

Stay away from *all* get rich quick, or something for nothing schemes as if they were poison - they *are*. Do not delude yourself with false and stupid concepts, words, ideas and opinions based on reifications - word *noises*. This is almost complete insanity.

Remember "energy in = energy out." If a scheme or plan offers the moon ($1,000,000 output) for $1.00

(input), it is insanity, not natural order and doomed to fail. Not only will it fail but those tied to it will pay a stiff penalty. How is the universe going to demand the payment of $999,999 you owe?

Just as your motor keeps turning *all* the time to make a complete journey, from start to finish, so you *must* keep intelligently at your work to have it bear fruit. Hitch you wagon to a fence post and *start* to dig!

Nothing stands still. The whole universe is in motion. You are either going forward or going backward. If you are not consciously going forward with your goals and plans you will be slipping backward even though you don't realize it. An old Egyptian saying: "go soft, go slow, go far."

And, if you value your sanity, well-being, good health and the possibility of a decent future, *get out of emotional thinking*. This blurs and darkens your *seeing* and *doing*, becoming blind, only catastrophe can result.

Your emotions have their proper place and structure in your life; they pertain to the feelings not to the thinking. Try as best as you can to do all your thinking without becoming emotionally involved otherwise it is like mixing oil and water; they don't.

Emotional thinking and a preponderance of emotional surges in your daily life *automatically* cause misevaluations in all your judgments. This acts as mathematically as turning the steering wheel of your car the wrong way and piling into another car on that side.

Emotions and thinking are two entirely different functions of your life. They were never intended to be mixed. You cannot get an intelligent evaluation when they are. You cannot correctly bake a cake by mixing sand and flour. Mixing these two will make you unconscious and can lead to accidents.

When emotions and emotional thinking control or predominate in your life:

- You leak vital energy fast; nothing is left to power your everyday living.

- You have *no* protection against illness caused by rapports with family, loved ones and friends. It may be that well over 80% of all sickness is thus caused.

- Your reception of sensory data from the outer world becomes weaker, blurred, distorted or else ceases completely in the blinding waves of agitated emotions.

- This also tunes you into thousands of others who are also resonating to these negative emotions. You can then descend into hell (out of tuning and confusion).

- You lose most of your shielding of the aura.

STEPS ON THE PATH

STAR MANNA 1

Dare to enter the Soundless Center
Where the speaking silence will be your mentor
Know the Truth as a resonant tone
To make you a god from a talking stone.

Clean your triangle of head-heart-hand
As a growing immortal then clearly stand
In Perception's space, and light and power
To cleanse the mind and structure the hour.

Drink from the silence its healing force
That activates link from being to Source
Tempered in suffering must you seven times aspire
That in you may light the Gnostic Fire.

From the triangle and circle to the cube and square
Through geometry's lens know the Eternal Pair
Of balanced force in balanced form
That the compass of your day trace the Eternal Norm.

Through Will, and Wisdom and Activity bright
Transmute the man-darkness to Supreme Light
That the spectrum of your night and day
Can structure your steps on the Eternal Way.

Isidore Friedman

EQUANIMITY: LET THE MIND BECOME LIKE A CALM lake, perfectly reflecting everything around it. *No waves* of images and thought-feeling.

Everything should be done *slowly, calmly, coolly, consciously*; realize *now* that what you are doing *at this moment* will be the seed whose fruit you *must* reap and experience later.

Train yourself *rigorously* in *all* that you say and do, so that:

- your mind is balanced
- your emotions tranquil
- your body is relaxed

Keeping the above three things in focus, become *conscious* of all around you; *and* the inner world of images-thought reaction.

All your life is a sowing-reaping; you reap *exactly* and precisely what you sow; neither more nor less. Then you *sow* what you reap as the seed becomes a plant and the plant generates more seed.

Your present (the NOW) is *both the flower* of the past and the *seed* (cause) in your future. *This is your life*, a constant seeding and doing *now*, and a constant reaping-experiencing in the as-yet-to-be.

To *allow* yourself to become unconscious of:

- what you are saying;
- what you are thinking;
- what you are feeling;
- what you are doing;

is to start committing *suicide*, either rapid or slow. Stay *conscious* for longer periods every day.

Pay *conscious attention* to whatever you are doing in the Here-Now - a whole different spectrum of insights, experiences, awareness, images and thoughts will enter and penetrate your field of consciousness.

Be *constantly* aware of the *speed* and *intensity* of your daily speech. It is almost always better to talk slower, softer and calmer than you usually do. Any time you get carried away by your speech and emotion-thoughts, slow down immediately.

It is difficult, but *extremely vital*, to become conscious of the state of your being; the *focus* of your attention, and your inner impulses; unconsciousness of these factors in everyday living usually starts forming negative spirals of force which lead to chaos and destruction.

Work slowly, sanely, by very *small degrees*, to get your attention, choice and decision under the control of your consciousness. To have the above controlled by the lower forces of the personality is to, sooner or later, be doomed.

Grow up or blow up; we literally have no choice. We either begin to learn the basic Cosmic Laws in both ourselves and the universe or we create in us the prison-hell of a confused and unhappy life through identification with the false pictures, goals, thoughts, emotions and concepts of our ignorance-steeped personality.

Your life is *fated*; your fate consists of your:

	ATTENTION
FOCUS:	TIME
	ENERGY
	DIRECTION

This is a mathematical formula - it ALWAYS works. Your life shapes up by, and grows into, how you use and focus your attention; how you use time, and direct your energy.

Dear Seeker, you should work hard to discover all the patterns of behavior, good and bad, that have been formed in your being through indiscriminate imitation. This mode of functioning corresponds to the moon, which, as it has no "light" (lacking in discrimination) of its own, "reflects" (reproduces, imitates) the "light" of the Sun.

ORGANIC NOTES

STAR FRUIT 1

After the pain, the muck, the ire
After the burning of the Gnosis Fire
After the cleansing of the verbal dross
Enter the rays from the Nameless Source.

The Heavenly Fruit hangs high and bright
Gleaming and golden on the Tree of Light
Made of Love and Power and Wisdom-Essence
A fragrant form of the Shining One's presence.

The seeing clears and knows on sight
The true, the false - the wrong, the right
Gone emotion's boiling trouble
Made from identity's sleazy rubble.

Punctured the drive for words' heated blight
The less the words, the clearer the sight
And CALM descends from the regions above
To make radiant healing that is Silent Love.

And Rhythm and Light form a patterned weave
That melts the course of the emotions' grieve
And Light, and Love and Wisdom-Power
Make golden and bright each daily hour.

Isidore Friedman

YOUR MIND DIVIDES INTO THREE COMPARTMENTS: the conscious mind (the one you are using now); the subconscious mind (the powerhouse - whatever you put into it that you get back); and the superconscious mind - another name for the Presence of God Who lives within you. The greater part of mankind is not aware of this.

You must work in the laboratory that is "you;" your thoughts, concepts, images, ideas, emotions, actions and speech. Gradually, *little by little*, you will both become aware of them, then control and direct them. Self-discipline in this is of the essence. *Important*!

The moment we stop trying to copy the next person and begin to realize who we are and what we are and what our potential is, that moment we are on the way to freedom.

You must watch *constantly* what you think - what is going on in your mind - *that* is making your future.

Your future is in your own hands; nobody is going to stop you but yourself.

The way to begin is to begin -
The way to begin is to begin -
The way to begin is to begin -
The way to begin is to begin -

The *root* of all true inner occult training depends mostly on:
- learning to *see* - without associations
- learning to *hear* - without memories
- learning to *speak* - consciously
- learning to *speak* - in and from the Here-Now
- learning to *register*; *not react*
- conscious, complete and constant self-mastery.

As we begin to clear out the debris of the subconscious, a slow growing awareness of the Presence begins to make itself felt.

How do we clear out this subconscious debris? Become consciously aware of the type of thought you hold and express most of the time.

A human is a microcosmic being, and any law of Truth that applies to the Cosmos applies to you.

Whatever you believe with conviction and/or feeling your subconscious will reproduce, or tend to reproduce.

The subconscious does not reason. It definitely has no sense of humor. But, it has a *complete* memory, as well as a record of anything you ever believed with conviction, carefully stored away. These memories it reproduces over and over until we begin to devise a way of controlling it and changing what we do not want there.

Remember, when the subconscious gets an idea clearly and concisely it will do everything in the world to reproduce it. It must always be properly directed; and it is equally powerful in either direction - for good or ill.

Nothing will happen to change your life until you consciously step in and start to work with the subconscious mind.

Otherwise, your old patterns will continue to manifest, and you will live your life at the mercy of the subconscious.

Watch yourself (in a relaxed way) all day - also *watch* your words, thoughts and actions. Stay kind, stay neutral, stay cheerful for more and more time each day. It will take time, discipline and training, but so does everything else in life that is worthwhile.

Relaxation is *urgently* important. Say to your body, "Be Still." Then lie prone on the floor for five minutes, on your back, without moving anything but the eyes and eyelids. Lie where you can watch the clock. Do this for five minutes a day for one week. The second week, lengthen it to ten minutes. At the end of this, you will have control over body.

If you repeat *any idea often enough*, it begins to make an impression, until by reiteration you pack it into your subconscious. Personality equals the sum total of your subconscious expression clothed in your consciousness.

We should recognize that each individual is a unique being and there is really no such thing as a norm. Until the subconscious pattern is changed, nothing will happen to change you permanently.

Anytime you have any sort of negative thought, word or action packed with feeling, into the subconscious it goes and before you know it, it has reproduced - and you wonder why. You have forgotten the time you put it there.

We often hear people say, "I can't drink coffee at night. It will keep me awake." Actually, coffee will never keep you awake, but your faith in the idea will. Faith is a *directed belief.*

Nothing ever happens to any one of us, and I am going to repeat it again and again. Nothing ever happens to anyone of us, good or bad, that we ourselves have not inspired, that we have not fathered. When we really face that fact, our entire attitude toward any problem completely changes.

Two of our greatest stumbling blocks are fear and resentment.

Our problems in a general way tell us what is wrong with the subconscious.

We build up our problems by thought; by thought we can disintegrate them. By changing our thought, problems begin to fade.

The subconscious knows what you believe in, and that is what you actually demonstrate.

The real meaning of the word love is "yoke" (Sanskrit). It is the nature of the subconscious that makes us cling to our problems, and that is the thing we must re-direct.

ON

SELF KNOWLEDGE

Awake!

Though walking and talking, we blindly sleep
Lost in the subconscious, mighty, deep
The future fear, and lament the past
Tightly bound to an image mast.

Wake from sleep of the living dead
Be awake, conscious, eat this moment's bread
Learn to hear, and be, and look
Drink deeply from the moment's brook.

Be conscious, aware of the Here and Now,
Thus soil of the future you safely plough
With healthy, wealthy, happy seeds
To grow to fruit to nourish your needs.

Isidore Friedman

A TRAINED, FLEXIBLE, *STRONG* ATTENTION SHOULD be the goal of anyone interested in penetrating the deeper mysteries of life.

Work consciously and intelligently at getting your attention *stronger* than any event, word, idea, symbol, thought, emotion or concept.

Everything depends on self-knowledge; anyone ignorant of himself will take anything (good or bad) and *automatically* create destructive things and acts and relations through unawareness.

Your creative imagination (picture-making faculty) *must* be controlled by reason, will and judgment. Otherwise, it will surely destroy you due to the tremendous *negative* suggestions from your environment.

Patience is the crown that securely holds the Jewel of Enlightenment - without her, all desire, knowledge and accomplishments will eventually lead to chaos and destruction.

A simple method of making over your whole life:

Stop! Stop doing wrong things. We all do wrong things, make mistakes, stumble, etc.; but the method of reconstruction is: simply to start doing wrong things then stop, *deliberately* - start impulsively, stop consciously.

We determine to watch ourselves each day; at the moment we become aware that we are saying, thinking or doing something wrong, let us say to ourselves, quietly and firmly: *STOP*.

Don't let discouragement enter in. When you find discouragement or any type of emotion or thinking entering in, firmly say the potent word *STOP*.

Two qualities are essential to sane living: *wisdom* and *detachment*. Without them we are mentally blind, and cannot rightly lead or be led.

If we be wise, we will discriminate sharply as to who and what we allow to teach us.

A man may be mentally wise, but not good; a man may be good, but his reasoning unsound. A book may contain many revelations mixed with much nonsense. Only *calm, patient* detachment can show the way.

One cannot accurately observe without emotional and mental detachment. There is nothing so blinding to true perception as emotional or mental involvement in the situation or person contemplated.

Right judgment can only come through compassionate detachment. The human element must never be left out of consideration. *But*, it must never be permitted to obscure basic principles.

We cannot truly understand if we do not maintain a warm and compassionate attitude in all human problems. But, maudlin and weak sentimentality is lacking in common sense, and is as harmful as is cruel and unfeeling withdrawal into intellective contemplation of the problem. One attitude is emotional blindness, the other is mental blindness.

Most of us fail because we try to do too many things too quickly and with too little preparation and thoughtful consideration. This is not a world where big things are done swiftly. We forget this and attempt too much. Slow, clear, calm and conscious should be your procedure in all things.

Your attention, choice and decision should be carefully pruned constantly; springing into action or speech on a blind impulse is not only wasteful and futile, it is *exceedingly* dangerous.

You have so much space, time, energy and matter available at any given moment. Too much incurs waste and confusion; too little does not have the force to overcome the natural resistance and inertia all around us.

RIGHT SPEECH

RIGHT SPEECH

Right speech, right glance
Order the animals/inanimate
In Life's Cosmic Dance.

Right tone, right state
In daily life
Grow strength and harmony
Without mindless strife.

Emotional thinking, the animal's way
Bestialize the mind, in Hell does one stray
Reason, Attention, and Order's Light
Heal body and mind, make everything right.

Isidore Friedman

BEFORE THERE CAN BE RIGHT SPEECH, THERE HAS to be right feeling and right thought. The person must be *aware* of his feelings, thoughts, the environment around him. He must also be aware of the other person's general feeling, mood and state of being.

He must *never* just say things unconsciously, automatically caught up by the stream of his own unconscious thought-feeling pouring into words, inundating and sometimes actually repelling the listener's sense of decorum and what is proper to the space-time continuum of the environment.

He should be continually aware of the effect his words and actions are having or could have on his listener.

There must be a disciplined, ordered, intelligent and steady practice of the law of three during the act of speech.

The speaker should ask himself:

Are my words-actions *congruent* (fitting, proper) to the context of the whole living situation between myself and the listener?

Are they directly and specifically concerned with the matter on hand - or are they non-sequitur?

Am I talking *too much* in the space-time matrix of the Now?

Am I putting *too much* emotional force into my words and so repelling my listeners or frightening them?

Am I using the proper language to fit the other person's manifold of speech and ideas?

Are my words too vague, unclear, spaced-out, or without a referent in reality for the other person to get a coherent understanding of my speech?

Am I offending the other person's sensibilities to any unconscious word, action or mannerism?

Am I getting to the point in simple, clear, direct and coherent language, and then do I stop? Or, do I keep rambling aimlessly using oceans of words and tiring and annoying my listener?

Do I make myself *aware* of the listener's state? Obviously, if he is in a hurry or has a scheduled appointment, I should respect this and structure my message accordingly.

Keeping people waiting needlessly, and unnecessarily has rung the death knell of many a doctor or teacher or public speaker's career.

Am I getting lost in the sound of my own beautiful rhetoric and so becoming unconscious of my listener's needs, responses, answers, etc.?

Do I keep my words under *strict control*, saving my voice, energy, time and efforts for the next things that I have to do?

Do I get so wrapped up in my unconscious flow of words that I lose *contact* with what my listener is thinking and feeling?

Do I become aware, that at certain times, my listener's mento-emotional state is such that he is out of contact with the Here-Now, and so is incapable of receiving my message?

Do I carefully watch the timing of what I am saying; am I aware of the ripeness or unripeness of the person's mind before me so as to mesh in properly with his needs?

Bluntly, do I speak too much?

Am I boring the person?

Am I using metaphors, analogies and comparisons beyond the reach of my listener's experience?

Am I relating my message and explanations *consciously* to my listener's experience and understanding?

Am I a compulsive talker?

All proper, helpful and healing speech is a balanced relationship between the sower (speaker), seed (words) and the soil (listener's mind). Be sure to link up *all* these three coordinates consciously.

Also, you must make allowance for a varied and interesting repetition of your basic points at different times; allowance should also be made for the gradual growth of your ideas in the listener's mind.

You must discipline your speech daily and hourly so that:

- Less words are used.
- Simple words are used.
- Pictures within the experience of the listener are used.
- Clear words are used and the speech is directed and controlled. Don't wander verbally.

Do I waste my time, attention and force on idle and unnecessary chatter?

Am I too personal in my relationship with my clients?

It is part of wisdom to:

- Never make excuses for yourself.
- Never blame another when things go off-key and wrong.
- Never get depressed over negative manifestations, nor elated over positive ones.
- Never permit your speech to get too positive or too negative - the returning backwash is usually very strong and often quite disconcerting.

Remember speech is an energy functioning in an energy pattern called a circuit, the circuit consists of you, the other person, the attention and the relations between - *all* the components are needed. Where one is missing the circuit gets broken, and the transfer of meaning and knowledge breaks down.

Talk slower than usual; talk softly; talk with rhythm and from a relaxed state of being. Tense talking or feeling pressured when talking makes the vocal sounds and speech unpleasant, ugly, repellent and can cause a destructive effect on the listener.

Do not give too much information at one time.

This tends to overload and then short circuits the listener's mind; make the communication pleasant, impersonal, friendly, short and to the point.

Don't MEANDER, WANDER AND CHATTER NON-SEQUITURS. This has a *very* negative and unpleasant feedback, either sooner or later, in unpleasant and unexpected and trying events.

Constantly be aware of the time-space, energy-matter co-ordinates of the present moment; if you do not lose sight of the Here-Now, much good will be seeded.

Experiences are unavoidable and necessary. However, the memories, fears, anxieties and hopes called up by resonating unconsciously with these vestigial shadows that experiences call up - these are not necessary.

These waste energy, add confusion, misdirect your forces, darken and make psychic shadows where none exist in reality - from these you must detach and free yourself.

Only then can you become free. Only through disciplining your mental and emotional moods and automatic responses can you tread the beginning road to freedom.

There is no possibility of freedom, insight and control of your life without training of your body, emotions, mind and speech.

Without intelligent, rhythmic, training of these factors in the natural order of the cosmos which sustains and maintains us, there is no other path but a negative descending spiral into chaos and destruction, while insanely mumbling high "verbal truths" and principles, as love, God and the divine universe, etc., etc., etc. Ad nauseum.

The emotional force of what is said can hypnotize people into attempting things and goals where there is *no practical factual ability* to perform the required steps towards the goal's materialization. This is pure delusion.

Everything in the galaxies, star clusters and universe materialized through a process of orderly trend - and functional sequence.

We, too, are a part of this functional process-sequence of an orderly universe.

When we violate these cosmic laws, either through ignorance, greed or delusion, we cut off the song of our life as certainly and surely as a radio stop playing when the plug is pulled out of its power source.

An omni-dimensional and omni-lateral approach to life, living and functioning is not just an interesting theory; it is an immediate and urgent necessity if we are to survive the stress changes from a tribal to a global life.

We are as much a part of a larger cosmic life as the fish are part of the ocean in which they swim.

In fact, just as fish are condensed ocean, we are condensed Star-Life, Eternity trapped, unknowingly, in a form-of-flesh which ignorance converts to a prison.

By knowing ourselves (our structure-function-order) and then knowing the larger structure-function-order of the cosmic process (God) which sustains, maintains and gives us life, we may gradually evolve out of the prison of form knowingly into a higher dimension of being analogous to a caterpillar cracking its cocoon, becoming a butterfly and then exploring this new dimension (air) with its new wings.

SOME FUNDAMENTALS OF THE NEW AGE GNOSIS

STAR SEED ALPHA 2

First, your Center in you find
then no outer creed can bind
Your thoughts and feelings, your actions free
To explore the sphere of Eternity.

Let no outer sight your vision blind
The perceptive clarity of your seeing mind.
Let no word or emotion make
The prison that does your birthright take.

Sell not your soul to idea or thought
Like a fly in tight spider's web caught
In pretty illusions of meaningless sound
In a verbal cocoon of darkness bound.

The Golden Phoenix of balance mount
To bring you to the Origin's fount
Of light and Love and Wisdom-Power
To transmute to gold the day's every hour.

To sing, in the dark, of your Founding Star
The true Light Being you really are
To struggle free of the word-made mesh
And in the Nectar of Light, your soul to refresh.

Isidore Friedman

ALL NATURE IS RHYTHMIC - A PULSATION between the so-called pairs of opposites on the different levels.

The basic rhythm-pulse of all life is: action-rest, eat-digest, go-stop, etc., etc., etc.

Most of our society today is exceedingly sick from being out of rhythm - or from trying to impose a mechanical rhythm, pre-set and occupational, on its members. Such a rhythm is not organic, it builds up an ever greater crescendo of tension, and winds up breeding all kinds of diseases: physical, emotional, and mental. It fosters imbalance.

Now, an unbalanced consciousness actually creates unbalance everywhere it goes, and in everything it touches.

From this unbalance, a negative force-field is created; from this reversed field comes a host of big and little plagues which bedevil our days and cause us sleepless nights.

Now, when we are out of our basic functional rhythm, or unbalanced for any reason whatever, we are passive (negative, receptive) to all the latent chaos in our environment.

By a process of magnetic induction, the chaos around us then programs our personal aura-field, like a data-processing computer.

We begin to tune in to, not only the chaos in our environment, but to all the chaos in the inner worlds of thought and feeling to which we are related by resonance.

Thus, when we get frustrated, angry, or depressed, we actually open the inner doors of our being to the wave-length of anger and depression. And ALL of that cesspool garbage that most of humanity is creating on the inner thought-feeling plane pours right into you, and takes over control. You are now only a cork on the bubbling, boiling rip-tide of chaotic emotional-mental force - driven towards negative happenings and different degrees of destruction.

The sheer volume of this negative force can destroy in one moment what has taken you years of constructive effort, toil, and sweat to build up.

When you have tuned into, and are immersed in, this negative force-field, you

- do not hear correctly
- do not see correctly
- do not touch correctly
- do not smell correctly
- do not feel correctly
- do not think correctly

- do not act correctly.

You are thus *completely* out of touch and rapport with your environment in the Here-Now of the present moment which is your link with eternity.

Consequently, your unconscious handling of your day's obligation, responsibilities and needs leads to catastrophes, in an ever-increasing spiral - plus exhausting your physical-emotional-mental batteries as there is not enough energy to cope with your environmental duties, pleasures, and exigencies.

The body is a battery; the mind is a tuning device. When the body energy is low or distorted, the mind *must* AUTOMATICALLY malfunction.

When the mind malfunctions, the body's smooth operation is interfered with, causing an even greater wastage of energy. This causes even more chaos in the mind - and the dwindling spiral of unconsciousness leading to hell (confusion) and ignorance (out of tuning) is entered upon - with disastrous consequences. So, the first step in breaking the chain of negative force-field is:

- *STOP!*
- Stop churning emotionally and diarrheaing mentally.
- Come back to the present moment.
- Take six or so deep, soft, slow rhythmic breaths.

- Wash your hands and face with *very* cold water.
- Take a good look at everything in your environment - look, don't think.
- Massage the back of your neck firmly.
- Yawn. Blink your eyes like a butterfly's wings.
- Laugh at yourself for getting caught up in nonsense, from a deeper, wider more inclusive viewpoint.
- Feel your cheek, nose, lip, hair with your hand.
- SLOW DOWN on all three levels - physically, mentally, and emotionally.
- Begin to establish control over your forces.
- In the midst of all this chaos, whatever you will do in an unbalanced state will only increase the chaos and its control over you.
- So, don't do. Put yourself in neutral, and begin to gather relevant and well-proportioned data - facts about the situation you are now confronted with, knowing that the calmer you become, the better will be the outcome of this 'crisis.'

You have begun to order yourself, which is the first step in ordering and controlling your environment.

Unbalanced energy takes a cosmos (order) and makes it a chaos (disorder).

Wrong focus, non-sequiturs, all push you away from your goal in the Gnosis of becoming a light-being.

Evil is that which pushes you away from your goal, good moves you towards it. You must select and choose consciously only those energy-acts, and thought-feelings which correlate with your goal. You must hitch your wagon to a fence post and plough your own field.

Wrong use of time is unconscious suicide. Your time is your life; proper use and proportion of your time will bring you all or most of your deep, heart-felt needs, satisfactions and goals.

You must learn to apply structure, order and system to your daily events and pattern of living.

System equals a space-time, energy-matter manifold; an ordered relation of parts-to-whole; and a definite, balanced, rhythmic sequence of action in time.

Your manifold equals your frames of reference and your system of evaluations. Your manifold determines your life, destiny, future and happiness-fulfillment as a conscious co-creator in the Cosmic structure-function-order-process we call God.

PERCEPTON

STAR MANNA 8

The Light, the Love, the Wisdom-Power
Seed each moment, hour by hour
With force and form linked by color and sound
And the Shaping Triangle spins round and round.

And births the tones into living tunes
Of spiral forms and deathless runes
To encode the Alphabet of Living Fire
To build a firmament's loving spire.

To hum the Alpha-Omega song
For seven aeons, seven eternities long
To form the formless into shapes of power
So that fire-seeds into gods can flower.

And work, as younger gods must and will
So Patterns of Light into the dark can spill
So the sleeping sparks can awake and wonder
At the Eternal's puissant ordering thunder.

Isidore Friedman

AND THEN PERCEPTON, SAGE-SCRIBE OF THE Wise Ones, See-er of the Light, Knower of the Truth, Doer of the Will-Wisdom-Activity Of the Shining Ones, Lords of Order, dipped his radiant pen made of patterned Noetic Light into the purified and healing blood of Wisdom, and then inscribed on Permeon, incorruptible substance of the records of Eternity, made of Eternity fleshed in form, of stable light from the Static Kingdom, these words:

Know ye, oh seeking ones, that before ye may walk in the clear, cool light of Eternity, tread the Wisdom Path of the Skyways, know and read the growing purpose of THAT which made the Star-Ways that, first you must grovel in the dust, then drink of the nectared light of the peaks, then again grovel in the dust - till, awakening to recognition of the Gnosis-Process opens the Triangled Eye of a most holy One dwelling in pain and suffering, in the most secret chamber of your mind-heart.

Having, after many aeons of untold suffering and quenchless thirst, burned away the dross ignorance-poison of the emotions, mastered the Wild Horses of the Sun lodged in your breast, brought to heel and to order most of the unbalanced forces in you that impede your steady motion to the light - having silenced forever the monkey-mind and its verbal, delusional rot - the blinding push of the passioned emotions ever ready to leap automatically into action and destroy all with the evil force of Unmeasure;

Having gained control and understood the function of the scissor mind working by imitation, comparison and unconscious thrust, with *no* linking to the Higher Forces; having learned by steady daily training, to silence the yammer of the lower mind, to remain calm in the midst of the boiling emotions of the less-than-human; having earned through untiring effort to guide and control the wild, ravening, destructive horses of unconscious, compulsive speech;

Having earned and learned the omnipresence of the Law of Three in manifestation; having walked on the edge of the Abyss of Ignorance and peered into its miasmatic depths, so often, and so calmly that its poisonous fumes no longer unsteady your nerves - having seated yourself in the Temple of the Undistracted Mind and the cool tranquil heart; having learned through effort and the conscious mathematical application of your understanding to ALL things; having done all this,

You may request, by the Law of EARNED EFFORT and the PRICE THAT HAS BEEN PAID, aid from the Builder Gods and their workmen the Shining Ones, to be shown the correct direction to face, to tread your way out of the whirlpool vortex of ignorance through identification with words, of the Greed-Hatred-

Delusion forming the prison bars of your ignorance made from this identification - safe from being driven, like a blinded pack animal, to destruction by the unbalanced forces around you and in you.

Always remember, O Seeking One, on this level, Awareness is God, your shield and protection from evil, your friend, companion, helpmate, guide and true servant who will stand you in good stead all through the chaotic voyages of your day over the roaring ocean and typhoons of unbalance. The root necessity for conscious balance and alternation is as great and urgent as for beathing, on this level, if one wishes to live and function in this form-of-flesh.

Light and Dark weave the alternate web on which the Loom of the Universe is sustained; both the positive and the negative forces have equal value in your deeper growth. The positive events bring rest, some fulfillment and joy; the negative events are stern but necessary teachers of courage, patience, strength and endurance. They also bring skill in the handling of cycles. Just as both sunshine and rain are equally necessary for the growth of good crops, so do the plus and the negative forces provide the needed nourishment, skill and opportunity for solid growth.

The busy pen of Percepton continued to glow with ever increasing light as it moved easily over the Permeon:

We live, move, and have our being in an Electrical Universe. In a certain sense, Nature can be called the constant oscillation between plus and minus (more or less), God could be delineated as the balance point or stabilizing factor. This function of the Triune God repeats endlessly, in numberless octaves, chords, scales, cycles, structures, functions and orders. To know and apply this is already Great Wisdom.

Spirit, soul and body might just as readily be translated as voltage, current and resistance, to set up an electrical analogue. Or, Spirit might be called the hub of the wheel, soul the connecting spokes, and the rim would be the body. The necessary functional inter-relationships amongst these three form a deep insight into Cosmic Order.

Everything in the universe exemplifies polarity; oscillates from more to less and vice versa; and radiates, penetrates and absorbs.

You are a whole composed of parts; on another level, you are part of a larger whole. Health, sanity, joy and reason consist of learning and forming your own chord - then, later, linking to the larger chord of the universe in an intelligent, purposeful, ordered and structured way. The Shining Ones and the Lords of Order need those who can become conscious co-Creators with them in the forming of Singing Universes and purpose-filled beings to work, create, serve and love.

Purpose, joy, meaning, love, and wisdom all lie dormant until the lessons and skills of tuning, toning, resonance, matching and natural order function are learned, assimilated, digested and become a constant factor in everyday living. Thus, can the orderly links in the cosmic chain of evolving beings be joined properly, and maintain an independent-dependency which becomes easily apparent when the level of being moves, by degrees, into cosmic impersonality.

Become a skilled craftsman; your mind and body strong tools, your daily events and functions the necessary materials on which your tools will work; shape them consciously so that the clear sight of meaning can filter through and make every job and event well done and a collector of light.

Imperceptibly but surely will your work and tone draw the attention of the cosmic builders; your mind-heart and entire being will become permeated with the force and light of higher spheres - giving you a taste of heaven.

You will teach, help, heal and serve by what you are; not by what you say. Your balanced doing and perceptive working will gradually diminish and finally eliminate the need and necessity for much speech. Bear in mind that speech and perception are in inverse ratio; the more you speak the less you perceive and know.

Much talk always indicates a person who is not balanced, is insecure within himself, and a more or less robot-puppet to run by blindly unconscious outer stimuli and/or automatic inner thoughts and feelings.

The form changes according to the nature of the obstacle it meets; obstacles met consciously mean victory and greater understanding; unconsciously met obstacles degrade the consciousness, darken the perceptions and destroy basic faith in ourselves, life, and the basically creative, beneficent and orderly workers of the universe. Obstacles met intelligently and in aware state help us shape our lives into the true forms of our needs, structure and consciousness.

Percepton stopped writing; his inner state transformed his magnificent face into a radiating field of light, wisdom, power and joy. The very air around him began to glow as an automatic reaction and reflex to his highly tuned state of being - the very atmosphere and everything in it became lighter, brighter, cleaner and more alive. A vibrant smell as of millions of good growing things permeated everywhere and his awareness transformed itself to audible beautiful music in everything around him.

Percepton then wrote: Space is alive and teeming with living forces in invisible and partially visible form. By the mere act of what and how you think, these forms begin to activate, localize, energize and approach you. Literally and factually, every man is drawing to him his future, good or bad, conscious or unconscious - just as you scrub and clean your hands before eating, or after a greasy job, so you might, daily, scrub and clean your mind from these buzzing, foul insect thoughts.

Think of Light often, little brother. Everything we see is basically light in different states and shapes and stages of condensation.

Matter is frozen light, needing but the touch of true understanding, synthesis and structure to show scintillating rainbow spectra of amazing and beautiful colors - one of the Great Ones has said that matter is frozen music, waiting only the touch of a skilled master hand to melt into harmonies sublime, ecstatic and soul-nourishing.

Let the feel and realization of the light that you are, and the Greater Light you are yet to become, lift you, and daily energize the higher frequencies of Light-Love-Wisdom-Power to enter the structure of your being and heal and regenerate you.

Bless the Light and think of it often, O struggler after meaning. In it are contained your health, growth, sanity and soul - nourishment for continuous growth. You are at heart, a light being - your vicissitudes and dark shadows are only portions of unconscious areas in you which have to be cleansed and removed by your growing conscious awareness, light.

Forms are the visible parts of God's nature made manifest - an ugly form not only is a sacrilege against nature, it also emits chaotic rays that detune and destroy, in various degree, all around it.

The proper structuring, creating and balancing of forms-filled-with-light is part of the godling's joy, need, duty, responsibility and means of growth into ever higher spheres of consciousness. Forms of light act as a kind of searchlight to pierce the black fog of ignorance held in so many minds.

Nature shows and teaches you all in the most obvious simplicity – man's distorted and complex mind makes complexity out of basic structure and pattern of cosmos. Thus, man's mind reflects back the broken and distorted images, like a broken mirror reflects back distorted shards of light from the original true ray.

It is man, whose word-and-associative mechanisms have gone out of control, who creates the chaos and disorder all around him from the basically ordered tendencies and processes in nature.

Man has become an animal run by his lower centers; until he lifts himself to the light, understanding and peace of the higher frequencies, he must toil, boil, and soil all in the hot, uncontrolled muck of his lower emotional centers which continually distort the true rays of light-forms meant to show and teach man his higher nature.

Ordinary life has been called "the mirror of the passing show." A mirror can only reflect a two-dimensional image and invert the reality which formed it in the first place.

The wild tigers of uncontrolled, automatic and blinding speech make true perception impossible. The words ring up automatic associations instantly and block sight; the emotions push-pull the being into hasty, perverted and misevaluated action, speech and thought; the heat and the confusion are compounded compulsively and impulsively; the person then sees incorrectly, hears improperly, judges wrongly, and then becomes furious because nothing turns out as he wishes and hopes. Next, he manifests anger-hate, then destruction.

Much strength calmly applied; a balanced mind earned in the daily heat of battle; the root ability to remain calm, unmoved and emotionally neutral in the midst of all this verbal, visual and tactile chaos must be slowly, tenaciously, and persistently structured into the being with patience, steady effort and conscious work. Then will sight and hearing come back to those who are blinded and deafened by the turmoil of the outer market place and the turbulence of the emotion-twisted heart.

Then wrote Percepton in letter of flame and light:

- Let the mind rest steady in the rays of the higher.
- Let the heart remain tranquil and undisturbed at the blinding and deafening reports of the senses.
- Let the hand work with strength, skill, rhythm and control at the blending of the triune forces of the true being.
- Let the breath be controlled, stable, steady and unemotional.

Then having established control over the unbalanced force at the root of his being - then and only then - can he, conscious and aware, be a living bridge between heaven and earth.

Then the seeds which were the golden thoughts of Percepton flashed forth on the radiant Permeon and became fragrant flowers of perceptive insight:

Words are but inadequate attempts at the lower levels of life: they have some meaning when structured and used properly; however, they block higher perception and the energy of light-meaning since they are only associative symbols - reliance on words-ideas-thought only leads to the pit of blindness and to those who crawl in the dark; as a being of light you must live in the clear-seeing of perception.

Percepton continued: Light reveals; love heals; wisdom binds the two into functional use and skill in action. Without knowledge of structure and polarized magnetic fields, words become empty noises and the mad muttering of mumbling monkeys chattering forth their fear, greed, hatred and complete delusion. Words that are not structured to specific situations are not only unconscious, meaningless abstractions, they blind and delude both speaker and listener and make the receipt of true structural knowledge almost impossible.

Percepton lifted his pen and rested for a while. Finally, he leaned over and continued:

Because of automatic listening one does not hear; through automatic speech one becomes blind and harmful to others; through automatic working, energy becomes wasted, perceptions go astray - one becomes a part of the mad crowd degraded continually by unconscious sensation and bored emotions.

The first business of consciousness is perception; after that comes clean, precise and accurate recording - then comes the work of thoughts, dogmas, opinion and the other twaddle.

Without clear referents for important words, confusion and misevaluation automatically take place. This then creates pockets of dissatisfaction, ignorance, frustration, futility which in turn lead to fury, irritability and finally overt acts of hatred and wrong actions in certain contexts of situation. These all fester, as negative magnetic impulses in the subconscious minds of people, who then, at the first outer stimulus, discharge in confusion and hate their prior negative conditioning and force-fields.

Anyone identified with, and run by, words, thoughts, feelings, concepts, dogmas, ideas, opinions, etc., etc., cannot see clearly, think clearly, evaluate properly. His input data processing circuits are out of order, physically and psychically incapable of truly recording anything happening around him. His measurement of things, thoughts and people will continually be off; he will himself be so unbalanced as to render null, void and impossible any clear, sane and proper judgment.

Percepton paused and listened lovingly to the joyous bird sounds permeating the perfumed air of the little forest garden wherein he was writing:

Patience and bare attention are the jewel seeds that make clear perception possible. Patience slows down the input data and allows the complete data entrance to the sensory circuits; bare attention permits the exact form, sound, sight and touch of the phenomena to modulate our bodily sensors and give adequate and clear recording from which perceptive judgment is made.

Without these two, the recording and storage circuits of the brain become short-circuited; actual microscopic cracks form on the surface of the brain and mind function becomes distorted. Once this happens it becomes functionally impossible for the brain to receive, store, combine and give back true facsimiles of what has been impressed on it, thus altering and distorting the life-facts which make clear and accurate judgment possible.

Percepton stopped writing and laid down his pen. It continued to glow, emitting pulsing concentric circles of light in an orderly pattern of peaks and lows. It seemed to be looking intently at Percepton with love and a desire to be of service to him.

Percepton then spoke, bringing joy to the hearts and light to the minds of all those listening:

Order, alternation and pattern are the three working tools by which the way of the Gods is first built, then traveled, persistently, unemotionally and intelligently. There is a structured order and nature pattern in everything that manifests. The perception of this, and its application practically to our everyday lives, the Gods call meaning and the path. Seeing, hearing, touching and sensing this meaning is one of the greatest joys in life. Through persistent, consistent, and trained effort, this skill will grow constantly, strengthening your heart and removing ignorance (the darkness of unmeasured, emotional thinking and identification) from your body-mind-soul.

Build a trained attention, a focused awareness (flexible yet strong) and a capacity and ability to sense, store, control, direct and regulate the varied energies, both within and without; both in yourself and in the environment around. Always remember that your thoughts and feeling-emotions are also part of your environment. Being unaware of your moods, thoughts and feelings at any time is tantamount to crossing the street in heavy traffic with your eyes closed. Catastrophe then occurs and people in their nescience call it an accident.

One of the first and most difficult steps on the path to light, (both inner and outer) is to gradually and by small degrees break the grip that unconscious thoughts, feelings, desires, opinions, ideas, platitudes and all verbalisms have on you. In the macrocosmos, we see constantly the outworking of an ordered rhythm, harmony, and melody which create the music of cosmic function. Similarly, in our daily lives, we must establish, (again by small degrees) an ordered rhythm, harmony and melody (based on our structure) in the microcosmos of our body-mind-soul.

This will gradually but surely begin to harmonize the various warring energies in us which prevent anything constructive from being built into our lives.

As these energies are harmonized by our understanding, need and will, we grow calmer. As we grow quieter, we can then begin to apply the cosmic principles of order, alternation and pattern more and more to our lives - thus bringing in more peace, light, love and wisdom to structure our lives properly as growing godlings.

Realize well, said Percepton, the battle against the ignorance of ingrained habits, an untrained mind and unconscious speech is constant, harrowing, extremely difficult and sure to be lost, unless we apply scientifically, the structure-function-order laws of cosmos; we must also constantly invoke the aid of the Higher Forces by shaping our lives into structured, balanced and harmonized forms so that the higher messages can enter our ordered receptor.

Anger, hatred, fear, worry and doubt are diseases of ignorance, lack of knowledge of the cosmic forces which keep us alive, sodden and bestial habits which form the bars of our prison cage; and sheer brute, animal laziness. Imperceptibly, in very tiny degrees, cleanse yourself from these defilements which cause malfunction, misery and pure hell in every level of your being, besides destroying all around you. Little by little, slowly, scientifically, re-structure your being and doing to become a small but good light channel.

Percepton smiled, and the buds of the plants around him immediately changed into full blown flowers, their perfumed fragrance filling the air with a delightful symphony of smell. Again, the music of Percepton's voice welled forth in rhythmic, cadenced and healing speech:

What you say and do become echoes which your environment then reflects back to you - sooner or later, but inexorably, you will have to face the fruit of events from the seeds of talk, thought and action which you yourself have planted and set into motion. Only in trained perception can you acquire the skill and the wisdom to choose correctly and in a cosmically balanced away.

Proportion, ratio, and measure, and their constant use daily, come next in order after you have focused yourself and your life in perception, rather than the chains of thinking-emotion-acting, all usually automatic, unconscious, over-reactive, unmeasured and out of control. These help make your prison bars ever stronger, and block the light necessary to see, and so to function.

In a quiet, orderly, relaxed yet focused stance, do what has to be done in your day. Refuse to dismount from the throne of dynamic balance at whose center lies strength, proper function and the coordination necessary to handle things properly.

Speak less, and softer, listen more, and from a quiet balanced mind-hear so you can really hear; refuse to act on all unnecessary and chaotic emotion-thought impulses. A measured survey and review will render these vestiges from the animal past quiescent and harmless.

Above all, become conscious; more and more, hour by hour, day by day. As these flow into weeks, months and years, you will find yourself happier and healthier - your days will sing with the power of order, and your nights become joyous with the healing knowledge of things well done, relevant and meaningful to your microcosmos and scheme of things. You will also have started the process of detuning yourself from the negative powers and forces that lurk in all unbalanced words, states, moods, actions, emotions, opinions, and ideas and procedures.

Arguing and justifying anything must be stricken from your life completely; pointless and aimless discussions over empty verbal forms which are mostly noises which enslave you to unconscious identification also must be extirpated: fascination with words and idea-mongering is not only useless and stupid, it wastes precious energy which is the substance of God force in you to mount the ladder of light - using and discarding ever more adequate force-forms, which, like exercise dumb bells, strengthen the muscles of your perception, attention, awareness and skill-in-everyday function.

You must acquire the skill and the capacity to build any idea into a form-of-force; to hold onto and strengthen it in constructive use; and to let it go immediately after its usefulness is gone because of time and a changing environment.

The more talk, the more the life energy is wasted; the more the unconscious talk, the more the unconscious speech is processed and laid into your mental computer as negative data programming - rest assured that conditions and events will, more or less, fall into line with this negative programming data, and make your life miserable and unhappy every day.

Superfluous and unconscious speech:

- waste life force
- thicken the ignorance in you
- waste time and opportunity for change
- create the mold and matrix for all kinds of illnesses, diseases and negative happenings.

Percepton then wrote on truth:

Truth, he said, on this plane is completely relative; it is proportioned; shaped and formed by the space-time, energy-matter coordinates then extant; it is always relative, and endures for a limited time always. It is for a period, a time, a particular space or place. Absolute truth on this plane is both the intellect gone insane and semantic suicide, both rolled into one; it is dangerous, inadequate, useless, false to the Natural Order and makes dogmatic fiends out of those who espouse it.

Truth is the knowledge of self and the not-self, and the relations between. And it is always relative to the space-time matrix which called it into being. Divorced from a context of situation and of relevance, it becomes a link of the strongest chain of lies imprisoning the seekers - pure, undiluted ignorance verbalized, then concretized by action into results which are false, deadly, anti-natural order and completely destructive.

Real truth may never be comprehended in a verbal form; it can never be completely or truly stated in a verbal form; it is hidden and disguised by a verbal form; but it can lead to some useful directions to explore.

After Percepton's last words, a restful, tranquil quiet placed its soft mantle of peace over all the listeners, both visible and invisible, and also over those of the intra-spaces of the inter-dimensional universes, numberless and ever growing.

Again, Percepton spoke and the trees, listening attentively moved their branches in soft approval:

In the real universes of energy, forces, forms, functions, and fields, there is a constant interaction and inter-penetration, interchange to nourish; to give and take in cycles of function, growth and dynamic change - whereas the world of words-ideas-opinions are all abstractions of an abstraction; unconsciously made, unconsciously evaluated and creating more delusion and chaos.

Percepton rested, withdrawn into the Noetic Field of Stable Light, fed and healed by the Brotherhood of the Golden Breathing Spiral; tired after the immense strain of being an inter-dimensional bridge between the world of light and the worlds of darkness - a cycle of rest and regeneration, and again Percepton grasped his pen and wrote on the glowing, eternal Permeon:

Many worlds have been created by the building tones of the Immortals, Guardians of the Light, channels and containers on the substance-forces of Light, Love, Wisdom and Power. These, my children, are not words and ideas, they are structured energy-forms filled with light-forces from the Higher Spheres; were it not for the eternal work of the Shining Ones in bringing down the sphere lights, all of humanity would long ago have destroyed itself, poisoned by the venom-death of its own ignorant emanations and destructive chaos-spawned force-fields. But now, many links to the higher have been destroyed by the Innocent Ones who are used by the Dark Forces to destroy the Light; this the Dark Forces well know, and so their influence, temporarily, seems to be increasing. This is one reason why Percepton, Sage-Scribe of the Wise Ones, and the Elder Brothers of the Golden Breathing Spiral have attempted the transfer of an adequate cosmic teaching in the language of man's contemporary environment. Improper language, Aristotelian thinking, and unilateral, blind (one sided) function are very real menaces to man's future and well-being.

Again and again, it must be reiterated that synthesis and multi-function, and the fact of our divine heritage as growing godlings are some of the most basic and important keys to the New Age now struggling so desperately to be born - the coordinates, parameters, basic multi-ordinality and structural functions are so completely different from the past, that without a solid, scientific, deep, strong and adequate training in the higher levels of being and function in the Here-Now, our present situation cannot be understood, fear will generate automatically, and hopelessness will engulf a majority.

This hopelessness, if allowed to grow unchecked, and if no compensating vectors of light and higher being are injected, can augment man's negative fears, doubts and animal proclivities to such a vast degree that man's self-destruction can become almost inevitable. On the other hand, if more of the godling sparks struggle ever more intensely, and pay the price of becoming Lighted Ones and receivers of the Higher Wisdom, Light and Power - and then WORK, indeed there can be much hope for a new and true beginning.

Percepton continued:

There is a singing joy in substance; a condensing of the Divine energies of the Higher Spheres - scorn it not, for the physical is a most wondrous bridge to the higher Forces. Just as white light contains within itself, the living spectrum of the rainbow colors, so substance contains, locked within itself, tremendous and glowing harmonies, substances, colors and tones - all waiting to be summoned forth by the trained mind, strong heart and skilled hand of the worker who is prepared and pays the price.

Just as substance contains these marvelous potential gifts, so in us are untold treasures, awaiting only right ordering, true pattern, and the focused efforts of awakened consciousness to begin to manifest degrees of Light, Love, Wisdom and Power in the higher spheres. What is needed is some kind of light engineering and celestial mechanics - the application of the Natural Order principles continuously and relentlessly to order and shape the chaos created by the millions of disordered animal minds.

Remember continually, O seeker after the energy of meaning and the light of purpose - you dwell in an ordered and scalar universe; everything that is, manifests in series of degrees - this in modern scientific parlance, has been called the Principle of Progressive Approximation (work growth and accomplishment by small orderly increments, by degrees, like a thermometer).

Thus, that which is congruent and proper to the times, the structure of circumstances, and the needs of the hour can be blended and developed through wise synthesis and the knowledge-application of the Cosmic Order.

Percepton's invocation to those who resonate to the seeding structure rhythms of his words, who dedicate themselves daily by their everyday functions to making of themselves strong and true and skilled channels for the light tones from the Higher infra-dimensional universes:

May you DAILY wake in peace walk in peace work in peace talk in peace love in peace rest in peace.

May the Light and the Love, and the Peace, and the Wisdom of the Golden Breathing Spiral Brotherhood enter and nourish and heal and cause to sing, in the power of true purpose, your mind, your heart, your nerves, your blood, the marrow of your bones and your entire being, as you tread the patterned way to the Light.

ISIDORE FRIEDMAN BOOKS

Organics: The Law of the Breathing Spiral

Songs of the Starlords

Organics: Practicing Bare Attention

Additional Isidore Friedman writings
Available at Pateron.com/spiritualfrequences

Vitvan Books and Audio Presentations available at The School of the Natural Order – Baker, NV
https://www.sno.org/

To learn more about Isidore Friedman and Organics watch and listen to the YouTube podcast *Tuning In* with Bob Lancer and Dr. Greg Nielsen – two of his students.
https://www.youtube.com/watch?v=BMryVGWWJZw

To Learn More:
Conscious Books
316 California Ave., Suite 210
Reno, Nevada 89509
Email: spiritualfrequenciesonline@gmail

About the Author

ISIDORE FRIEDMAN was born in Brooklyn, New York in 1917, an old soul with many conscious past life memories, he knew of his spiritual mission by the age of six. It was then that he began his deep studies of math, science and the wisdom of the east, subjects that would later be synthesized in the teaching he called Organics. He also took up piano, becoming a skilled and highly creative player. He specialized in the jazz of the forties and even invented a system of chord cards that teach improvisation. People remarked on the energy in his house, how calm and clear it made them feel, like having deep stresses released or coming out of a fog. Being around him was a pleasure, bring a sense of inner space and freedom. He was interesting to look at too. Though of Jewish roots, his face had something Hindu, Tibetan and Spaniard in it made one think of other places, other times. He had deep dark brown eyes that glowed with the light of kindness and awareness, a light that seemed to grow even brighter as the years passed by, just as his being grew wiser and peaceful. Sadly, in 1991 that light went out in this world as Iz passed over into the next one after a brief illness, leaving behind his legacy of wisdom and the beautiful memory of a life lived in truth and service. Since then, he is greatly missed by all who knew him, and more loved and valued than ever for he was unique and irreplaceable, a true sui generis.

Milton Keynes UK
Ingram Content Group UK Ltd.
UKHW021357011224
451693UK00012B/884